BATTLE

TO THE TOP

BATTLE
TO THE TOP

How to Become an
ACHIEVER
in the World of Finance

JASON BLACKWELL

RED DAGGER
PUBLISHING

Published by Red Dagger Publishing, East Hampton, NY

Edited and designed by Girl Friday Productions
www.girlfridayproductions.com

Cover design: Megan Katsanevakis
Project management: Reshma Kooner
Editorial production: Abi Pollokoff
Image credits: cover © iStock/bgblue, © iStock/VikiVector

ISBN (paperback): 979-8-9871904-0-1
ISBN (ebook): 979-8-9871904-1-8

I learned a lot about leadership from my time in the military and a lot more through my years as a coach. But nobody has taught me more about leadership than my daughter Mila. This book is dedicated to her.

CONTENTS

INTRODUCTION

The sweat was beginning to pour off me. I had over eighty pounds of equipment strapped to my body, and I was less than fifteen minutes from Iraq. The chemical suit I was wearing would protect me from the nerve agents we were told Saddam Hussein would unleash on us, but it meant I was boiling inside. I had been in the back of this helicopter over thirty times on numerous mission rehearsals, but I had never sweated like this.

It was 18:45 on March 20, 2003, the first night of the Iraq invasion. I was attached to a group of thirty US Special Forces, most of them from SEAL Team 3. We were packed into the back of the MH-53 Pave Low, one of the world's largest helicopters. The tension was building by the minute. You could see it on the faces surrounding me, illuminated by the strange, eerie green light of night vision goggles.

Our mission was to secure an oil compound on the Al-Faw peninsula in the extreme southeast of Iraq on the Persian Gulf. This is where Iraq pumped most of its oil to offshore platforms, where it got picked up by massive tankers. There was intelligence that the Iraqis planned to blow it up once the invasion started, to flood the gulf with oil, putting a halt to any coalition invasion. My mission was to go in with the SEALs, secure the compound and the important infrastructure, and set up two helicopter landing sites to bring in the first UK soldiers from 40 Commando Royal Marines, one of the UK's most elite units, into Iraq.

We had been receiving daily intelligence briefings for six weeks. The intelligence guys were utterly confident they knew the exact locations and numbers of the enemy.

How wrong they were.

***

I looked to my right and saw one of the crewmen, who was standing right behind the pilots in the doorway, staring at a small note the pilots had passed to him. He looked at it and handed it back to me. I turned on the small red light attached to my jacket zipper and read the note: "not 24 enemy, 124." In other words, we would face about five times more enemy troops than the intelligence team had told us about.

I took a deep breath. That news was not something we were expecting. The intelligence guys had made a mistake, but there was nothing I could do about that now. There was no point even giving it a second thought. My job was to focus on what was to come, not what had happened.

I passed the note to Chris, sitting directly to my left. He was a United States Air Force combat controller, whose job would be to direct all the aircraft we would have to support our mission onto targets. He quickly scanned the note and then promptly passed it to his left. He looked up at me. He had one of those little smiles you put on when you know things aren't great. But he also had a look of complete control. We all had it: no panic, just focus—we had trained hard, and we all knew we would deal with whatever was thrown at us.

I was suddenly hit by a huge dose of reality. We were going to face a big fight; there was no chance that 124 enemies would surrender. People were probably going to die.

***

At 18:50, we turned away from Iraq and entered a holding pattern over Bubiyan Island, between the coasts of Kuwait and Iraq. I was in the lead helicopter with seven other MH-53s trailing behind in formation. The eight helicopters were low, about one hundred feet above the water, and flying close together.

We took turns looking out the small window on the right-hand side of the helicopter. The firepower of the United States Air Force was still taking out enemy antiaircraft and command positions around our landing zone, using a combination of cruise missiles and a B-52 bomber dropping its huge payload.

We were supposed to land at 19:00. It was getting later and later, though, and there was no sign we would be landing anytime soon. Time had gone relatively quickly since we had taken off from Kuwait two hours earlier. Now every minute was beginning to drag.

The overpowering odor of the explosives—which comes from the cordite in the bombs—permeated the aircraft, filling my lungs and nearly making me choke. I sat back on the floor, staring into the darkness at my feet. I envisioned Prime Minister Tony Blair making speeches to the nation about the battle while my family hung on his every word, not realizing the severity of my situation. I had fleeting thoughts of my family, wondering if they would receive a knock on the door tonight with news that I was one of the dead. It was nearly five o'clock back home in Dorset, in southwest England, and I pictured all my friends back at the air station where we were based, probably enjoying a cup of tea, maybe driving home from work.

I was a couple of months into my deployment to the Middle East, and, perhaps selfishly, I had not thought of home that much. Maybe that was mental and emotional self-defense. It was easier to hide from the suffering those at home were experiencing than face its reality. I felt enough pressure in the current moment without adding to it from afar. To be successful in the mission, I knew the best choice was to focus and clear my mind of unnecessary distractions.

Because of the size of the helicopters and the number in the formation, we were sitting ducks until the antiaircraft weapons on the peninsula were taken out by the air strikes the coalition forces were sending in. Being a sitting duck in a war zone is never a good thing. I kept thinking if anything were to happen, I just hoped it would be quick and painless.

The back of the aircraft was so dark that I could only make out the guys sitting around me. The looks on the familiar faces had changed during the two-hour flight from Kuwait, from friendly and relaxed to ones of pure focus.

***

At 18:55, another message came down from the pilots. Surely this couldn't be more bad news. It wasn't. Our landing time, known as H hour, was now 19:15. Twenty more minutes to endure this hell.

Although the situation was difficult and the stakes could mean the death of others or myself, I would not have swapped my position for a massive lottery win. I had spent my entire career in the military preparing to be in this position. It's a bizarre thing that people in the military must contend with. We spend years training for an event that may never happen. You may never get the chance to test yourself in actual combat. I saw myself as lucky, really lucky, to be in this situation.

Even still, at the same time, I felt the incredible pressure and reality of where I was. All I wanted was to get out on the ground, where I could at least influence matters.

The smell of the bombs grew stronger; the cruise missile and B-52 strikes had stopped, as the Iraqis' antiaircraft weapons we were most scared of had been taken out. Now two AC-130 Spectre gunships—which are the most fearsome aircraft you can have supporting you—armed with a frightening array of weaponry took over and started to clear enemy positions. I could only imagine the destruction over the peninsula. Young Iraqi soldiers who had probably only ever seen firepower like this on television were now experiencing firsthand the military might of the coalition.

We continually prepare for the unexpected throughout our training, to keep us sharp and on our toes. We will make equipment, such as a weapons system, fail at a critical time, or we will block an access point into a building and have to find a new way in. It ensures we can cope with any eventuality. I knew the situation could change in the blink of an eye. It wouldn't go as smoothly as we had hoped. The increase in the enemy's number was evidence of that. So I kept staring at my feet, attempting to stay focused on the mission. I ran through what I was going to do over and over in my head.

Back at the US Special Forces headquarters in Kuwait, I knew everyone would be surrounding a large plasma-screen television with a live feed from a USAF Predator drone that was flying over the peninsula. They would be watching as I flew into enemy territory with America's best. I had lived and trained with these guys for six weeks, and we all knew each other well. This was no rehearsal; there was a real enemy down there, and I was about to face them for the first time. I had waited for my entire career to be in a position like this. I was ready.

***

At 19:08, another note came down—H hour was definitely 19:15. There were other coordinated attacks, so we couldn't continue to delay. Most of 3 Commando Brigade, the elite fighting force of the British Royal Navy, was sitting in Kuwait waiting for the green light to fly into Iraq upon the successful completion of our mission.

Securing the oil compound would set off a chain reaction—the boats of 539 Squadron would land on the beach, 40 Commando would fly into my location, and 42 Commando would land to the north a short time after. At the same time, 29 Commando Royal Artillery would shoot their targets, giving us cover fire throughout the night.

***

At 19:10, the aircraft dove even lower toward the ground, and I could hear the enormous engines powering up. I could no longer think about home. I could no longer think about anything but the mission. We were now flying incredibly low, at only about fifty feet. I stood up and looked out the window again. The whole peninsula was on fire.

The stench was still overpowering. The guy in front of me put two fingers in the air—*two minutes out.* I was completely in the hands of the pilots now, but I trusted them to deliver us safely to the target, and I had to believe they would.

I dropped down on one knee, bringing my weapon to bear. Suddenly I felt incredibly calm. I was hit by a wave of peacefulness, as if I had already accepted the inevitable. Whoever was up there was now in charge of my fate.

I started to think of all the people who had ever pissed me off. I did not want to die with any regrets or hatred, so I forgave every one of them. It gave me an overwhelming sense of well-being. If only that feeling of release could be bottled and sold over the counter, it would heal a lot of anguish in the world. A wide smile broke over my face; the guy next to me must have thought I was a fool. I looked around and saw that most of the guys were grinning. I had no idea what thoughts were racing through their minds, but I knew I was prepared for whatever came next.

My peace was shattered as a single finger was waved in front of me—*one minute out.* My heart rate shot up. It must have been at maximum, and I could feel it thumping in my chest, but there was nothing I could do to calm it now. But while my heart raced, I felt in control, with complete clarity of thought.

I stood up and caught a glimpse of the coast as it flashed

past the window; I could even pick out small waves hitting the beach. I felt terrified and excited at the same time. I saw the oil compound for the first time, which I had previously only seen on satellite imagery. The 250-foot-tall communications tower in the center of the compound went whizzing past.

The aircraft then heaved over to the left, and we all went flying across the cabin. The pilot took no chances with a gentle approach; he went in at full speed. There was so much weight in the back of the helicopter, with all the troops and equipment, that the engines were screaming with the effort, and the noise was deafening. As we entered the landing zone, the helicopter's nose pitched up violently to take some of the speed off, and dust and sand flooded the helicopter. I pulled my goggles down and covered my face with a cloth called a shamag.

The aircraft slammed into the ground, and everyone was flung down again. The guys around me started yelling and shouting, psyching themselves up as the back ramp went down. Someone hit the back of my helmet and yelled, "Yeah! C'mon, fuckers!"

No choice now—I was going for it.

I had never felt so alert; my eyes were darting about, looking for signs of the enemy. I could see a stream of men ahead of me pouring out of the helicopter and disappearing into the dust cloud. Seconds later, it was my turn. I ran the length of the aircraft and down the back ramp, and my right foot hit the ground.

I was in Iraq.

***

My military experience was some of the most monumental of my life, and I wouldn't trade a second of it. When I got home to Dorset from Iraq, I needed to clear my head and reset. I found myself a bit lost. I remember going to the grocery store and staring at the milk in the cooler for what seemed like an eternity. A few days earlier, I was in Iraq; now I could buy 2 percent milk and go for a coffee.

I decided I needed to be alone with my thoughts, reflect, and figure out what the next chapter of my life would look like, so I went for a weeklong walk by myself through the mountains on the island of Corsica, off the south coast of France. Everything looked to be at an inflection point. Things seemed to come together and give me a sign it was time to move on from the military—I had just turned thirty, I had been in combat, and I had finished my university degree. So I submitted my resignation, and a few months later, I walked out of camp for the last time. I wanted to try something completely different and decided to complete a postgraduate course in journalism. I met a lot of journalists in Iraq, and it seemed to tick all the boxes that I thought I needed. It was exciting, adventurous, and challenging. I wanted to give it a go even though it was a million miles away from what I had done before.

Thanks to the contacts I made in journalism, I was lucky to be asked if I wanted to go to Beirut and write for the *Daily Express*, one of the UK's major newspapers. I jumped at the chance, and once I got there, I also wrote for other British and US newspapers, even appearing on Sky News and CNN for brief stints. Although I had experience in war-torn environments and an education in journalism, it wasn't a good fit. I loved the action and the thrill of witnessing world-changing events, but I wasn't very good at it. I remember reporting and researching stories in Beirut and trying my best to make them relevant for a UK audience, but then I'd submit 1,500-word stories to have only 100 of my original words left after the editor had gone through my work. The theme was there, the story was there, but that was about it. I had the humility to recognize that journalism wasn't meant for me and move on.

I flew home from Beirut and went to live on my family's farm in Northern Ireland for a while. I had no idea what to do next. I tried to think about what made me tick and what I enjoyed, and one thing that leaped out was my fascination with leadership.

I don't think I really knew it at the time, but when I look back now, I can see the huge amount of satisfaction I got when the opportunity to develop people arose. During this period after journalism, I left the UK and moved to America. I was lucky to meet someone in America who was an executive coach and needed help . . . and I found my niche. Sixteen years later, I have been coaching financial executives and other leaders for longer than I had been an officer in the British military. My coaching, as well as my service in the British Royal Navy, has given me a unique insight into the skill set and mindset needed for leadership success in the modern world. My military experience shaped me in ways that never would have occurred had I taken a business path alone. My advice has helped countless clients exceed their goals, and I have been drawing on my vast experience to help my clients achieve more than they thought possible.

Through insight, observation, reflection, and strategies I have learned along the way, I have developed a formula I refer to as the ACHIEVER method, designed to be a clear and simple path to help people be the best version of themselves.

Here is a high-level overview of each tactic:

Action—You *MUST* be ready and committed to taking action to become an ACHIEVER.

Communication—Communication skills are critical and unfortunately often overlooked.

Humility—A leader can only learn when they are humble.

Insight—Reflection and insight are lifelong skills that will serve the accomplished leader throughout their lifetime.

Emotional Intelligence—Not understanding emotions can destroy the most accomplished leader.

Vision—The world is continually changing. If the leader doesn't have a sound vision of what success entails for themselves, their lives, their families, and their relationships, they will find themselves in reactionary mode as life challenges present themselves.

Execution—Ideas without a sound execution plan will lie stagnant.

Resilience—Success is not easy, but it is accessible for those who are willing to grow, adapt, and strengthen, regardless of the challenges they face.

Why is it called ACHIEVER? I suppose some old habits die hard. When I put my military hat back on for a brief moment, I must admit that acronyms serve a purpose. They help the listener grasp and recall a concept quickly, ensuring deep learning and adherence.

The leaders I coach are already strong achievers. They may have been number one or two in their academic class or, at the very least, in the top 10 percent. They are used to competing and winning in most circumstances.

Unfortunately, the biggest blind spot in the corporate world is leadership training. The focus always seems to be on technical training. Get someone good at their core job, and once they get to a decent level, give them a team to run—no surprise that it doesn't go well, with no thought given to how good they are as a manager or leader.

Leadership skills, often referred to as soft skills, are glossed over or just assumed to be present. Soft skills are not easily quantifiable or measured. This gap can create a crippling weakness for financial leaders. They are used to success, sometimes within minutes, in the financial markets. But I understand through my time in the military that learning leadership skills takes time—and they need to begin on day one. In corporations, employees may not learn leadership skills until they've been working for ten years or more; some never do. I see and experience this void every day.

There's a common misconception about the military. I was somewhat shocked to learn that a civilian thought I could just give someone an order, and the soldier would follow it. I'm laughing a little as I share that with you. If there is no trust, there is no action in the military. No one, and I mean no one, will follow any leader they do not believe in. Leadership starts with the individual, and that individual is accountable for their decisions and actions. If leaders don't set a good example, they will find themselves on a solo journey. In the military, lives can and have been lost because of poor decisions and sloppy behavior. No one wants to be part of a deadly, unnecessary mistake. It starts with personal accountability. Once a person demonstrates trustworthiness, their teammates will be fiercely supportive, but not until that trust is earned.

Those who make it to an investment banking firm, a venture capital firm, or a financial consulting firm have likely achieved their entire life. They consistently won academically, in sports, and probably in the world of work too. They had to compete fiercely to get their job. They may be wondering, How do I maintain this level of success? I assure you that there is no way to take your financial career to the next level without mastering leadership skills. Leaders who sail by without learning these skills eventually self-destruct. History is filled with examples of failed leadership and its consequences. We don't have to look far to find someone who ruthlessly climbed their way to the top to then fall just as fast—and hard.

Unfortunately, many don't realize how essential these skills are until it's too late. Some of the people I work with are reluctant, wondering if they even need this kind of training. But I've seen it time and time again. If they don't gain leadership skills, they will hit a wall and struggle to get to the next level in their career.

I've used the best of my military experience, life experience, and coaching experience to develop the ACHIEVER model to help those working in finance make it to the top. Throughout the book, I will break down each concept and provide actionable steps.

Now that you understand the basics of the ACHIEVER method's concepts, it's time to dig into each tactic.

Let's get started.

A—ACTION

There are risks and costs to action. But they
are far less than the long-range risks of comfortable inaction.

—John F. Kennedy (1917–1963)
Thirty-fifth president of the United States

O ne of the first questions I ask of a prospective client is
"Are you coachable?" At the heart of that question is this:
Are they ready to take action? Implementing the ACHIEVER
method to win the battle to the top is not theoretical work.
The concepts outlined in this book cannot merely be studied
and understood. They must be acted upon.

What you will learn here are often referred to as *soft
skills*. They are "soft" because the skills are difficult to define
and cannot easily be quantified. There is no test to accurately
assess who has command of these skills or to know what they

need to work on. But these are skills you can attain through lifelong learning and awareness, which is critical because the world continually evolves and changes. We must change with it.

Unfortunately, these skills are glossed over or not taught at all in many education systems. I find that many of the accomplished professionals I work with have to start from the ground up. Here's an example of one of my clients who hit a plateau in his career because he dismissed the importance of soft skills.

Barrett hadn't been promoted for three years in a row at the venture capital firm where he'd worked, despite being excellent with clients. It was almost as if an entirely new person emerged when the client spotlight shone upon him. He was charming, attentive, focused, and productive. That behavior, however, was only reserved for the people whom he wanted to impress.

In contrast, no one else wanted to be around him, from the receptionist to the junior analysts who worked on his deals. His peers grudgingly tolerated him. He was so demeaning that he couldn't keep an assistant, not even one he paid for out of his own pocket.

Of course, it was never Barrett's fault. His favorite term to describe anyone who didn't meet his exacting standards was *slacker*. Somehow, no one could read his mind or agree to be available on demand or anticipate his every whim well enough.

I conducted an informal 360-degree review and spoke to a few people who worked with him, during which I heard words like "condescending," "abusive," "arrogant," and "explosive" to describe Barrett. Dillon, the partner who'd sent Barrett to me, told me that he didn't think much of coaches and consultants; however, he wanted to retain Barrett. Dillon had founded the successful venture capital firm just ten years earlier and finally realized that he'd reluctantly have to let Barrett go if things didn't improve. Sending him to me was a last-ditch effort. It was either that or maybe a lawsuit.

Generally, I'm up for any challenge, but it was clear to me based on my assessment that Barrett was not interested in outside perspectives. He knew it all and was ready to blow through our interview. Our conversation lasted about thirty minutes. He hardly made eye contact and constantly glanced at his phone while we were talking.

I asked Barrett the question I ask everyone I work with: "Are you coachable?" He told me he was, but he doubted he needed it, even calling people who do need coaching "slackers"!

"I can't work with him," I said to myself as I left his office. I can count on one hand the number of times I have said this in my coaching career.

I then called Dillon and said, "I don't want to waste your time or money. I can't help here; he's neither ready for help nor wants it."

Thinking this engagement was over, I moved on to other, more pressing work. Later that same evening, I received an email. I was surprised to see it was from Barrett. The email read as follows:

> Jason, would you reconsider working with me?
>
> I returned home and told my girlfriend that I was assigned to work with some coach as people in the office had been complaining about me.
>
> I told her that our meeting was a waste of time when Dillon called. He said, "Barrett, this isn't working. I don't know what else to do."
>
> When I hung up the phone, my girlfriend pointed out that meeting with you was probably supposed to be a wake-up call. Apparently, I didn't get it.
>
> I'm now willing to listen. I'm ready to learn. I've asked Dillon to reconsider until I've given your program a fair shot.

I stared at the message on my phone for a minute. I wasn't expecting this, and I wasn't planning on working with Barrett. This assignment would be like doing surgery without an anesthetic.

Barrett had zero personal awareness and no concept of the implications of his actions in the office. I anticipated he wouldn't receive my messages well. However, he stated that he was willing to listen, which is fundamental to taking action.

I'm here to help people achieve their goals, and not just the easy ones. If I could turn Barrett around, I'd really get to put my system to the test.

Barrett suffered from what I call a deep perception gap. How he thought people saw him and how they actually did were miles apart. He felt his success-spotting and investing in potentially profitable start-ups was all there was to be a thriving venture capitalist. I'd seen this issue before but never to this extent. He had established zero trust with his colleagues and had a problematic reputation. Dillon was slightly aware of the struggle with Barrett but gave his people, especially his successful leaders, autonomy to do their jobs. This happens a lot in financial firms. Those who consistently generate revenue are often forgiven for what management sees as minor transgressions. The universe of what constitutes a "minor" transgression tends to grow in proportion to the revenue. Investors loved Barrett's gift for spotting the unlikely concept that would turn into tomorrow's next tech transformation. That's why Barrett had survived for so long. But at this point, his behavior was too egregious for Dillon to give Barrett influence over the company as a managing partner, which was the logical next step in his career.

Barrett was a very savvy financial professional with a high IQ, but either he was completely unaware of all the work that was going on in the background to fix all the turmoil his actions created, or he didn't care. This led to low-trust relationships with everyone he worked with. Nobody knew which version of Barrett they would get from one day to the next, which made everything more difficult. To paraphrase Stephen M. R. Covey in his *New York Times* bestselling book *The Speed of Trust: The One Thing That Changes Everything*, we have a "trust bank account" with everyone we meet. If we break the bond of trust in any situation, it will require substantial deposits of trustworthy behavior to mitigate one transgression, even when the oversight is unintentional. Barrett's trust bank account was nearing bankruptcy.

Regardless of all the obstacles, I decided Barrett was worth my time investment, and as you've probably guessed, I like a challenge. The glimmer of hope that he could become an ACHIEVER was his increasing awareness that his actions and behavior were part of the problem; the fact he was willing to write the email to me and hear some outside advice was the clearest signal he could have sent. The risk of losing his shot at managing partner and his only advocate, Dillon, forced him to pay attention. His girlfriend's insights likely got his attention as well . . . I think she may well have used the opportunity to tell him some home truths too! The perception gap was beginning to narrow, if only slightly.

Our road was going to be a long one. Barrett would need to learn to be accountable for his behavior, and he would have to be open to hearing messages he didn't like and acquiring skills he'd been dismissing for years. The tools I teach are not complex, but they are challenging to absorb and apply. They take time, investment, and humility to learn. As stated previously, not many people get what it takes to understand and implement the soft skills outlined in the ACHIEVER method. Soft skills are difficult to detect when used with proficiency. Not only that, but my clients have often been dismissive of soft skills. They've been trained to measure success through spreadsheets and the bottom line. What they fail to see is that soft skills are the foundation and the connective tissue that enable individuals to thrive. Soft skills can indeed be subtle, but a lack of them is glaringly and often painfully obvious.

From my personal experience, I was deeply influenced by a British general called Peter de la Billière. DLB, as he was known, was the British leader alongside American general "Stormin' Norman" Schwarzkopf in the first Gulf War in 1991. He had an incredible career and was a highly respected leader in the regular army and Special Forces, where he ended up leading the UK's elite Special Air Service.

I was a couple of years out from entering Dartmouth, the British Royal Naval College, and was constantly glued to the TV screen during the buildup to the actual war. I knew the military was in my future, and this was essential viewing for a budding military officer. DLB was larger than life, extremely direct, and exuded charisma and confidence—exactly what you want from the leader deciding your plan of action. I remember witnessing DLB's command of a room during a press conference. I watched him glide into the room, prepared and focused on his mission of giving a military brief, much of which contained difficult news. What really stood out to me was that he took the time to greet each staff person by looking them straight in the eye, warmly acknowledging them, and shaking their hand before starting. He had so much responsibility on his shoulders but still had that human touch. Through actions like that, he defined military leadership for a generation of young men like me. I also began to realize there isn't one style of leadership that is better than any other. DLB was the polar opposite to Norman Schwarzkopf, but both were equally amazing leaders.

After a brief follow-up conversation with Barrett, I was convinced he was willing to listen and was newly motivated. He wanted to reach the level of managing partner, regain Dillon's respect, and maintain his relationship with his girlfriend. The first rung on the ACHIEVER ladder of success is *action*. Barrett was ready to take that action, and I couldn't wait to get started now that I knew he was ready.

Barrett's turnaround was remarkable. We stayed in touch after the six-month assignment came to an end, and I saw him for the first time in person when the pandemic slowed down. He is now a managing partner, and Dillon is talking about retiring and promoting Barrett again. And yes, he is still with his girlfriend—she's now his wife.

***

If you want to become an ACHIEVER, there is no way to avoid taking action. Use this book as a tool kit: reread it and practice the tools, even when you don't quite grasp them yet or are skeptical of their efficacy. If you can't get to the next level in your firm, then you've picked up this book for a reason. By getting through the opening to this book, you've started to take action. The battle to the top is clearly outlined in the ACHIEVER method. I know it, I've used it myself, I've practiced it, and I help others get there. Grab a journal, a tablet, or the technology of your choice, and start your personal assessment. Budget enough time to give this exercise the attention it deserves.

ACTION STEPS:

✓ Describe yourself. Where do you excel? Where are you weak? Who likes you? Why? Who doesn't? Why? Do you exhibit any behaviors you dislike? What have you done about it? If nothing, maybe it's time to take action!

✓ Be accountable for all the negative relationships you have at the office. What have you done to derail those relationships?

✓ Build a relationship map. Don't dismiss anyone because of their title or role. Everyone has influence. Think three levels deep. With each connection, identify three of their subordinates, three of their peers, and three people who rely on their performance. How strong is your trust account with each person in your relationship map?

✓ Which leaders do you admire? Why? What is it about them that makes them excel? Choose one trait, focus on it for one week, and then choose another. What could you do to be more like them?

C—COMMUNICATION

It's a terrible thing to look over your shoulder
when you are trying to lead and find no one
there.

—Franklin D. Roosevelt (1882–1945)
Thirty-second president of the United States

M any people assume a great communicator is an impressive orator or presenter. I disagree and think it goes a lot
deeper than that. Great communicators do more than speak
well; they inspire and connect with their audience. They also
actively listen, read the room, and are aware of the emotions
of their audience.

Without effective communication skills, a leader is going
to have difficulty building a unified vision for their team.
There's a distinct difference between a leader and a manager.

The leader's role is to create the vision, build a plan to execute it, and then get the team's buy-in, all while maintaining the integrity of the organization. A manager's job is to execute on a task. Simply put, managers tell people what to do; a leader inspires them to do it. To be an ACHIEVER, you must learn to lead—simply managing tasks will only get you so far.

Leaders fail when they do not communicate clearly and set expectations with their team. They know what they mean; they know what they said. However, they often have no clue whether their team internalized those messages. Communicating is more than just speaking. In the same way, listening is more than just hearing. When communicating with others, the first thing I recommend you do as a leader is to ask yourself whether you clearly outlined your expectations. If you think you did, how did you do so? Did you take the time to precisely define what a successful working relationship or outcome would look like?

Here's a simple but common example—how quickly do you expect someone to respond to your emails? How often have you found yourself frustrated when you sent someone edits to review, and they have not sent them back in a couple of hours? Did you clearly outline when you needed the edits back? Your direct reports will falter every time if you expect them to anticipate your needs or intuitively understand your requirements. Ensure your team knows your expectations in each communication you send, whether electronic or verbal. Your version of "ASAP" or "the end of the day" might mean something very different to you than it does to them. These simple mistakes can lead to confusion, frustration, and conflict.

It's also imperative to be aware of how your communication style is perceived. Be wary of what I call the Wedding Speech Syndrome. Have you ever heard a memorable wedding speech? I can count the excellent wedding speeches I've listened to on one finger. Most of the time, a member of the wedding party will drone on and on, sharing inappropriate or tedious stories about the newly married couple. The crowd will be over the moon when the speech is over and they can return to the bar. But when the person who gave the speech walks over to the bar, people will lie and tell them how great it was. Make sure you get feedback from someone you trust who will give it to you straight, or you will fall victim to the Wedding Speech Syndrome.

Here's how to make sure this doesn't happen to you. After a client meeting or an important presentation, ask for honest feedback from those you trust, and be prepared to listen and act upon their comments and suggestions. Someone who works under you may not feel comfortable giving honest feedback, so seek out those who will. Likely it will be peers or supervisors who have a vested interest in making sure you succeed.

Effective communicators will know their communication style preferences and the preferences of those they are communicating with. Many assessment tools are available to help people become better communicators and listeners. At the core of communication style and preference is personality. Some of us are more direct (I certainly fall into this category). Some are more circumspect. Still others are more analytical and will stay quiet until they have all the information.

One of the tools I frequently use to gauge personality and communication style is the DiSC assessment. The acronym DiSC stands for *dominance, influence, steadiness,* and *conscientiousness,* which are four easy ways to categorizing people's communication styles based on their personality. This tool aims to show you your natural leadership and communication style and highlight the pros and cons so you can be a better communicator and flex your style to work with different personalities. It is important to note that not every communication style is the same, and part of success is staying true to your own authentic style. In my experience, when I see someone has copied someone else's style, it stands out and never looks quite right. I have seen numerous people try to present like President Obama or Steve Jobs over the years, but they always look like they're mimicking or copying these other leaders instead of being themselves.

The American psychologist William Marston (1893–1947) created DiSC after analyzing people's behaviors and communication styles in everyday situations. Interestingly, Marston was credited with creating an early prototype of the lie detector test, and he also created the superhero character

Wonder Woman. But his biggest coup, in my opinion, was the way he communicated content in a simple, straightforward manner, one that the layperson could easily absorb.

Here's an overview of the definition of the characteristics contained in the DiSC assessment. Even without taking the test, I bet you can self-analyze and put yourself into one of these four buckets. And if you can't, then ask someone you trust to help you do it.

> **D—Dominance.** People with this trait think fast, move fast, and act quickly. They don't want to hear all the details. They might cut you off mid-sentence. They like to get things done. Eighty percent certainty in any situation is good enough for them.

> **I—Influence.** Individuals with this characteristic enjoy being around and working with people. They enjoy hospitality, casual conversation, and getting to know the people they work alongside.

> **S—Steadiness.** Individuals who prefer this type of communication will want all the facts and processes laid out. They will be slow to take risks; they like a stable job versus working on a project or commission, regardless of how great the financial reward is.

C—Conscientiousness. This person has a healthy skepticism, and they enjoy working with numbers and data. They'll want to know all the details of how things work and what processes are dependent upon each other. This person will read an entire contract, highlighting and questioning along the way.

One of the critical notes about DiSC, and every other assessment tool, is that even though you will likely gravitate toward one particular style, you may display some of the characteristics of the different categories. Someone is rarely a pure *S* (steadiness), for example, without exhibiting any traits of the other types.

Each communication style has its strengths, and each one also has weaknesses. If you are aware of your communication style, you can develop a plan to leverage your strengths and minimize your weaknesses. Even for the most self-aware person, their strength may pivot into a disadvantage when under stress. People who are driven and passionate can become unstable and volatile. Those who are introverted and quiet can become more withdrawn. Perhaps a *C* (conscientiousness) overanswers and goes into the weeds, annoying everyone around them during the Q&A portion of a presentation. When we blow up and use our strength without awareness and diplomacy, our behaviors will backfire on us. We risk alienating the people we are attempting to engage.

Once you recognize your traits, you'll start to identify the personality traits of others. This awareness will become a great asset when leading teams. The person who is a high *D* (dominance) is wise to partner with a high *C* (conscientiousness) when negotiating contracts. Since the high *D* does not have a natural gift for thinking things through, the high *C* personality type may save them grief and minimize risk.

I'd like to tell a story illustrating the DiSC styles. Four people with different DiSC traits go to a restaurant. There's a long wait at the host stand. The *D* (dominance) starts demanding service, noting that empty tables are available. The *I* (influence) plays peacemaker, talking to the others in line, cracking jokes, and getting everyone laughing. The *S* (steadiness) stands off to the side, patiently waiting for their table. The *C* (conscientiousness) silently observes the situation, calculating the restaurant's lost revenue while mentally designing a more efficient process.

None of the above situations are better than the others. What is important is that you know your own natural style and its positive and negative traits and how to communicate with others who may have different styles.

Understanding your style will help you develop empathy for others. Understanding things from another person's perspective is an important leadership and communication skill. The person with empathy and understanding will recognize that each person in the restaurant line is waiting for the next empty table and is just being themselves. Individuals with self-awareness of their communication style will understand how their behavior affects others and adjust their behavior accordingly, which is a critical skill. Once you master this, you'll find yourself reading a room and quickly adapting when introduced to new groups of people.

For example, if you are someone with a dominant style, you will tend to drive the conversation and do most of the talking. This awareness allows you to examine how the world might see you: as someone who is always talking and not listening much. That is not a good trait for someone who is working with clients, as they may see you as someone who never shuts up to listen to others' opinions, or as someone who is overly aggressive. To set the stage for success, you might even give an overview of how you like to do things and ask others about their preferences. People love to be listened to, especially by their leaders. Listening sincerely to what is important to those around you is vital in building trust, and building trust results in sound working relationships.

Empathy will also help you read situations with deeper insight. If a teammate says they are willing to help, yet they subsequently do not answer your emails and are frequently unavailable, their actions are telling you something. As their leader, it's your job to determine what is going on. The reason they may not be replying could be personal. Perhaps they are struggling with the technological tools they are required to use. They may be receiving inconsistent messages or conflicting directions. It will serve you well to remember that no response *is* a response. When there is no response or a response you find unusual, make it a priority to find out what is going on, and address the situation head-on. Understanding a situation from another person's perspective is the definition of empathy.

Think of the last client or senior management meeting you attended. What was the style of the person sitting opposite you? Did you go into too much detail and bore them? Did you overanswer a question and go off on a tangent? This world contains a vast diversity of people, and we only get to know them by listening and learning. It's impossible to listen when we are talking. A wise person I once met told me we have one mouth and two ears for a reason.

Savvy communicators choose their words carefully and speak with intention. Spending most of your time with others listening to, assessing, and observing what they're saying is time well spent. It's easy to slip up; human nature dictates that we want to be heard. When we're speaking, we perceive we are in control. Be conscious of whether you are genuinely listening or just waiting for your turn to talk. A helpful acronym to remember is WAIT—Why Am I Talking?—when connecting or communicating with anyone.

To help answer this, ask yourself some additional questions: Am I blowing off steam? Processing my thoughts? What do I expect the listener to do with the information I'm sharing? Am I asking questions? Learning? Clarifying? Assessing? If there is no good answer to why you are talking, you're better off using your time to listen instead of wasting it by talking.

Listening also means allowing others to speak. Listen without judgment, and seek to understand versus correcting the speaker or redirecting their thoughts. Cutting off another person's sentence before they express their idea is annoying and is especially risky if they are a client or a senior leader. Time with clients and senior leaders is precious and tough to get, so don't spend it being rude or talking just for the sake of talking.

If you have an urge to finish another person's sentences, or if you hear yourself talking, take a deep breath and remember to WAIT. By thoroughly listening to others' perspectives, you stand to learn more than you ever could by talking your way through a conversation. Listening to people also builds trust. When your team recognizes that they are being heard and you care about their opinions and ideas, they will be eager to help you succeed, knowing that it will be a team win.

I learned about WAIT the hard way. I remember standing in line in the food tent in the Kuwait desert a few weeks before the war started. Next to me was a one-star British general, also standing in line and waiting his turn like all the rest of us. I thought we had a fantastic ten-minute conversation while the line slowly snaked toward the food. But it was only after I sat down to eat and reflected on it that I realized that I did all the talking. He was a master communicator and knew by letting me do all the talking that I would walk away thinking it was a great conversation. His wise use of listening enabled him to get insight into the pulse of what the men were thinking and learn their opinions on day-to-day matters.

The next time you have a casual conversation with a colleague or a team member, practice what the general did. Ask questions and listen. Open-ended questions will get more information than closed-ended questions. Open-ended questions start with "Tell me . . ." or *who, what, when, where, why,* and *how.* They will prompt the person you are speaking with to share more information. Closed-ended questions, which procure one-word answers, won't give you as much insight. "Did you have a good day?" can be answered with yes or no. In contrast, "Tell me about your day" will give you much more insight into what the person is experiencing. When you want to provide an opinion on the day's news, stop yourself; instead, ask the person you are with for their opinion and hear what they have to say first.

How much do you know about the people you work with? You might think you know them well. To illustrate how little team members know about each other, I often ask a group I am coaching to think of a team member they work with frequently. Once they have someone in mind, I'll ask, "When is their birthday?" Sheepishly one or two will chime in with an answer, although they'll admit the teammate's birthday was just last week. Knowing your teammates shouldn't stop at birthdays; understand what is important to them: their hobbies, family life, and goals and aspirations. People will flourish when they feel like they are part of a community where their colleagues and leaders care about them. I think of this quality as leadership charisma. People will never forget the leaders and contributors who sincerely cared about them.

I am frequently asked for advice on how to communicate better. Over the years, I have passed on a lot of strategies. Breaking it down into specific settings will help you overcome the many traps and pitfalls inherent in communication.

GOSSIP

It's best to rise above malicious talk, although it's not always easy. You might find yourself engaged in an unproductive conversation without initially realizing it. But there are ways out of the hole if you have sunk to these unfortunate depths.

An easy rule to follow to discern whether you are gossiping is to ask yourself, "Is the person I'm talking about present in the conversation? If not, why not?" Be honest as you assess whether you are venting. If you need to vent, talk to someone outside the system who has nothing to do with the situation. A coach is a good idea, but so is a good friend or family member. Venting is healthy and necessary. We all need to do it occasionally; however, attacking someone's character can damage a career.

If someone wants to gossip with you, you can deflect the situation by saying, "I get that's frustrating, but I don't want to gossip." A gentler approach is to ask, "What are you seeking from me? Are you asking for constructive feedback?" Both these tactics work and will stop ineffective communication immediately.

If you are in the position of listening to someone vent, keep the confidence. Don't repeat the detrimental information you hear. Take the time to learn for yourself whether the information shared is accurate. Could there be an extenuating circumstance you don't know about? If the colleague was venting to you, acknowledge what they experienced, and point out something positive about the person or situation. We can always find something positive if we look hard enough. Keeping confidences, especially in tenuous settings, will also help you build the coveted leadership quality of developing trusted relationships. We do not always act as our best selves. It's great to know you can be counted on as someone who "has people's backs" even when they slip up.

VIDEO MEETINGS

The global pandemic of 2020 made video meetings the new way to work and collaborate, and it won't go away anytime soon. Businesses, universities, and many other social groups shifted to using videoconferencing platforms to interact and run their businesses. Videoconferencing even became the new way to socialize with employees and friends. Zoom, one of the most popular meeting platforms, has become the go-to term to describe all virtual platforms and has been instrumental in the "new normal" sparked by the COVID-19

pandemic. Zoom has become so commonplace that people will say "let's Zoom" even when they're using a different
videoconferencing platform.

Now that we are well into using videoconferencing, fre-
quent users are starting to notice the psychological consequences of spending so much time on these video platforms.
Virtual burnout and exhaustion are commonplace, and
"Zoom fatigue" has taken hold, as many struggle with the side
effects. Stanford University researchers have developed the
Zoom Exhaustion and Fatigue scale, also known as the ZEF
scale. Their studies identify four primary causes of this newly
developed fatigue:

- **Eye contact**—The relentless eye contact from
  multiple parties we experience on virtual calls
  can induce stress. At the same time, we view the
  up-close faces we encounter on these same calls
  as subconsciously invading our personal space.
- **Self-viewing**—When our self-view cameras are
  turned on and visible on our screens, the constant reflection of ourselves often leads to increased self-criticism and, with that, stress. None
  of us sit in face-to-face meetings staring directly
  into mirrors, but this is precisely what we are experiencing on virtual calls.
- **Limited mobility**—Physical movement is frequently associated with improved cognitive

function; however, the stationary nature of Zoom allows little movement and can result in cognitive impairment. Even in the office, we move from room to room; now, we sometimes sit in the same place for hours.

• **Body language**—As humans, we rely on verbal and typical cues when communicating. Zoom calls offer a limited perspective of others' body language, requiring increased cognitive focus to interpret nonverbal cues. This, in turn, leads to increased fatigue.

Many more factors contribute to our Zoom fatigue, but the research indicates that if we focus on strategies to combat these four, we are likely to reduce the fatigue we are feeling. So what can we do about it?

The first thing to decide is whether you need to use video-conferencing. Remember when we all picked up the phone occasionally? It's still an option. Don't automatically default to video; first, determine whether it's even required and, if not, start to bring back audio calls and mix it up a little.

I encourage you to develop policies of your own for effective meetings; show some leadership. If something isn't working, there's usually no reason you can't change the policy to enhance productivity. If we gained anything from the COVID-19 pandemic, it's that we learned to question norms and find new ways of doing things. As an example, one of my clients has banned videoconferencing on Fridays to give employees a well-deserved break from it.

THE HYBRID WORKPLACE

Hybrid workplaces also evolved during the pandemic. Some people found saving their commuting time and working remotely was highly productive, while others suffered from the lack of collaboration being together as a team provides. As you lead your team, make sure you understand what they need for maximum productivity. Communication is a crucial issue when leading team members in a hybrid workplace. One of the many concerns is an "us versus them" situation where in-person workers receive clear direction and remote workers risk missing out. To avoid this, pay attention to these key four factors in the hybrid environment:

- **Inclusion**—Make sure all your team members have access to you. Do remote team members feel included and have an equal voice on the team?
- **Isolation**—We've discussed getting to know your team; this is never more important than when they are remote. Do team members feel like a team? Do members in remote or home locations feel disconnected?
- **Burnout**—Are you delegating? Keeping their home situation in mind, are people being given

the flexibility to accomplish tasks in the way that works for them? Burnout is just as much of an issue for you as the leader, so be aware of your workload too.

- **Clarity**—We know good communication is critical; make sure team members understand what the team's purpose is. Hold weekly team meetings to ensure everyone understands the simple things: workflow, who is heading out on vacation, and who is covering. Are there any upcoming projects you want them to be aware of? Are priorities clear?

Creating an intentional work environment in which team members can perform at their optimum level will make you a sought-after leader. When people understand that their success is your success, they will want to go above and beyond to help achieve and exceed goals.

IN-PERSON MEETINGS

Don't waste the opportunity to communicate with your teammates in face-to-face meetings. You'll be able to see everyone's body language and facial expressions. If someone looks concerned, confused, or angry, ask for clarification to learn whether they are giving physical cues that reflect their thoughts. Quiet people are sometimes introverts, and they might just be processing information. Make sure to draw them out by asking questions so that you can benefit from their input. Face-to-face meetings are an ideal time to build strong relationships.

The way you look is also a form of communication. The workplace is much more casual these days, and most people seem to enjoy the practicality of comfortable dress. However, I'll give you a piece of advice that I was given at the Naval College that will steer you in the right direction—*dress one level up*. Whatever type of meeting you are participating in, ensure that your attire conveys your authority. This becomes particularly important if you are hoping for a promotion. Dress for the level you want. This advice is more complex these days, rather than the classic navy suit with a white shirt and red tie for men and a conservative outfit like a black or navy pantsuit for women, so look at those above you and see how they dress.

When you call the meeting, identify the expectation and ensure everyone knows it. Will decisions be made? Are there various options to examine? This will stop people from going off on tangents and discussing things outside of the meeting's scope. Create an agenda and provide it to your teammates before the meeting. Ask if there's anything they would like to add. If it's possible and appropriate, add their suggestion. If not, explain why and make sure you address their concern. Quality meetings are intentional. Stay in control during the meeting, show leadership, and ensure everyone is involved.

EMAILS

One risk with email is that it's often misused for critical messaging. But it has enormous advantages, too, as it allows for
quick dissemination of information and the ability to receive
fast responses. Email enables streamlined business processes
and collaborative problem-solving. However, there are two
significant downsides to email. First, it never goes away; people can—and do—pull up emails from a decade ago. Second,
you have no idea to whom the recipient is showing the email.

My first piece of advice is to *never* send an email when
you feel even slightly emotional. In fifteen years of coaching, I
have yet to see an email that could not wait fifteen minutes—
and many times, if the situation is heated, it's okay to take a
business day to respond.

Here are some practical tips to make your emails more
effective:

- The subject line draws the reader in—keep it
  short, action based, and to the point.
- The opening line should state precisely what the
  email is about or describe what action is required.
- Call to action: be clear about what you need
  and, just as importantly, when you need it—your
  "ASAP" or "in due course" might mean very different things to the recipients.
- Use the appropriate tone. Be polite, direct, or

casual when needed. Think of the personality of the person you are emailing. If they are always polite, be polite back, no matter your current mood. If they are usually direct, bring your tone down a notch.

• Don't try to cram every detail into an email. Use bullet points when you can. If your fingers hurt while you hammer the keyboard, it might be time to stop and pick up the phone.

• Many messages are read on mobile devices, so craft your email to make it easy to read on a small screen.

• When crafting emails, I use the acronym ACT:

   A—Action. Make sure your email has a point. What is it about? The content should also be in the subject line.

   C—Context. Why is action needed? Explain why this needs to happen or why you are communicating.

   T—Timing. Take the initiative. Avoid "let's chat sometime" or "as soon as you can"—make the ask specific.

INSTANT MESSAGING

I was in a meeting where a participant thought he was sending a private message to a colleague using the chat function in

Zoom. While another of his colleagues presented, he wrote, "This is so boring," thinking it would be going to one individual. Instead, he hit Send, and it went to everyone in the chat. I'm sure he's still trying to rebuild credibility with his presenting colleague even now. Be careful, and use the tools of instant messaging thoughtfully. There are so many different instant messaging technologies out there now that it can be hard to keep track of how different platforms work—it's easy to make mistakes. While using an instant messaging platform like Slack or Bloomberg Chat can be informal, remember you still represent yourself and your brand. Keep it professional. Save the jokes for another time.

PRESENTATIONS

Giving a presentation can be daunting, no matter your level of seniority. Peers and clients are judging you, and it has not been uncommon over the years for executives to tell me how anxious it makes them.

After coaching thousands of people on how to present, I've collected a few tips:

- **Control is everything.** First, control your emotions. If you are not aware of how presenting makes you feel, those emotions can destroy how you present. For the next week, focus on your emotions just before you present. Are you

feeling anxious or nervous? Only once you appreciate your emotions can you control them. If
you feel nervous or anxious, breathe deeply and
relax; focus only on the first sixty seconds of the
presentation.

- **Control your delivery.** Use pauses to allow the
  audience to digest your message. Lose all the filler
  words and let the audience come on the journey
  with you.
- **Know your audience.** What do they care about?
  Focus on a message that will grab them.
- **Use visuals wisely.** Design PowerPoint presentations with select images and minimal bullet points.
  You wouldn't take a script to a movie and read it
  while the film rolls, so don't show your audience
  your script or simply read it out loud to them.
- **Practice your presentation.** Record it so you can
  hear the tone of your voice and recognize where
  you might stumble.

Don't make the mistake of taking the art of communication for granted by winging it. Vital leadership qualities
are showing up and being reliable. If your teammates can
trust your communication, it's a decisive step toward building trust, an essential leadership quality. By committing to
mastering these skills, you will be standing on a solid base on
your path to becoming an ACHIEVER.

ACTION STEPS:

✓ Communication is a vast, far-reaching, fluid web. Use this chapter as a reference and commit to honing your skills.

✓ Do some self-analyzing. What is your personality, and how does it affect how you communicate and interact with others? If you're not connecting with someone, take some accountability and alter your style to see if that helps.

✓ Remind yourself of WAIT (Why Am I Talking?). If there's no good reason for you to be talking, commit to listening. Post the acronym somewhere prominently where you can see it during meetings to remind yourself to listen more often than you talk.

✓ Evaluate yourself. How are you doing? If you think you're doing great, try listening again. We all have blind spots. Don't get trapped in the fallacy of the Wedding Speech Syndrome. Are you really good? Or is the audience just glad the speech is over? The more we listen, the more we learn.

✓ Your emails are representing you—use ACT to make sure they have impact and focus.

H—HUMILITY

I never fail; I only win—or I learn.

—Nelson Mandela (1918–2013)
Revolutionary, anti-apartheid activist,
president of South Africa

G etting comfortable with failure will open up your whole world, and I've had plenty of experience with that. Learning how to get comfortable with being uncomfortable and being open to learning something new is what humility is all about. The fact that you're holding this book in your hands is a good sign that you are willing to go on this journey. Humility equals flexibility. Those who are inflexible will only make it so far in their careers before they reach a dead end.

We often believe that we are exuding confidence by not

showing any weakness. But not showing any flaws is a sign of arrogance. I learned this lesson the hard way.

In 1999, I was a young, newly minted Green Beret. I had just passed one of the most demanding courses the British military offers, and I proudly wore the Commando badge on my arm. After a couple of weeks at my new unit in Yeovilton, Somerset, in southwest England, I was sent straight to Bosnia.

A corporal led the team for a couple of weeks before I arrived to take over. The three-person team already knew the country and had a rhythm of working in place before I came. They were seasoned operators with an average of six to twelve years of experience. So here I am, a twenty-six-year-old, freshly appointed Green Beret who has arrived to oversee and lead this established team.

Unfortunately, humility was not one of my core leadership qualities at this point in my life.

I had waited for my entire career to take and pass the Commando course. I felt as if I were GI Joe. At the time, I thought the Commando badge on my arm meant I had to have all the answers—or at least *act* like I had all the answers. I didn't want anyone to think I didn't know my stuff or couldn't lead this team. I was sure these experienced team operators would be able to spot any weakness from miles away, which only strengthened my resolve to show them I had it all together. There is no doubt—*I was pretending.* I was inexperienced, not only as a commando but in the theater of operations.

We were still at our unit base during my third day in Bosnia, waiting to go up-country on a job. I was in the officers' mess with some of the guys I knew from our camp back in England, but there were several new people there as well. There were two women in the group, Laura and Mary, who were in Bosnia for a few days to manage logistics. It was early evening, and the women said they would go for a run before dinner. Laura asked if I would like to join them.

Since I was in the best shape of my life at the time, I was eager to get out and get a workout in. And impressing a couple of women helped to seal the deal. The camp had a two-mile circuit around it, so I figured a couple of laps would be great.

I was fit and ready for anything. I thought, *I'll show these girls what I'm made of.* Our run, however, would turn out to be a little longer and a little more challenging than I anticipated, and Laura was about to teach me an important leadership lesson. We got about a mile into the run, and Mary started lagging slightly. Laura asked, "Do you mind if I keep this pace going?" and Mary said, "Go on ahead. I'm going to do my own thing." I stuck with Laura. I started to suspect this run would be longer and faster than the gentle jog I anticipated, and I was right. When I got to about the third mile with my running companion, I was starting to struggle to breathe. Laura was flying while I was barely keeping up. *I just finished Commando training; there's no way I can let her beat me,* I said to myself. At this point, I was gasping, doing my best to stick to her pace, while she was cruising along, chatting away, enjoying herself during a pleasant early-evening run. I was grumbling to myself, as I thought I should be killing this run. When we hit the end after only four miles, I was doubled over with exhaustion.

I could hardly walk and barely talk, and drool was escaping from both sides of my mouth. Laura was looking great; she was ready for another run. I gave her a quick wave as I tried to save face, gasping out the words "Great run! I enjoyed it!" She looked at me tentatively, asking, "You okay?" "Yeah, yeah," I assured her, thinking, *I'm okay . . . and ready for this experience to be over.* She went off to the women's quarters, and I walked back into the officers' mess. One of the guys said, "You all right? You don't look so good."

"No, I'm not. Just went out for the run from hell!" I explained. He asked who I went with, and when I told him Laura, he replied, *"Laura?* You know she's the army cross-country champion, right?" Laura was an Olympic-level athlete. No wonder I felt so wrecked.

I bumped into Laura that night at the bar after dinner. "How are you doing?" she asked. "Did you enjoy the run?" I assured her I did.

"You've got a green beret, right?" I nodded, and she replied, with a smile on her face, "Yeah, you've mentioned it a couple of times." I was mortified, embarrassed, and ashamed of my behavior. I looked at her and apologized. "I'm sorry,

Laura. You must think I'm an idiot. All I've done since I met you is talk at you and, even worse, try to impress you with my recent achievements. Can we start again?"

Laura was wonderful about it. She laughed and said of course we could. I held out my hand and introduced myself: "Hi, I'm Jason, I'm from Yorkshire, and I have a habit of talking too much."

Laura had taught me a great lesson by taking me on that run—she showed me that humility is a key attribute in not only a leader but a human being. It was a lesson I needed before I made a similar mistake leading my new team.

Instead of suggesting a run, she could've sat me down to talk about my behavior, but I likely wouldn't have listened. Today, the subtle, powerful way Laura pointed out my limitations sticks with me. All these years later, I remember Laura's leadership lesson and her willingness to invest time in me to point out how defeating my attitude was. I learned that I didn't have to walk around talking about my accomplishments. *Not talking about it and not drawing attention to it would have been more impressive than shouting it out. The team in Bosnia whom I was leading did not care that I had my green beret. For them it was nothing more than an entry to their world. After all, they all had one too. It is the same in finance. No one needs to hear about the college you went to or where you worked before got you the job. Instead, be humble about your past and show what you can do now.*

A big ego has a way of catching up with you. Being humble

may not seem like a prominent leadership attribute, but it is. Technical skills alone will not prepare you to climb the next rung on the ladder if you don't embrace humility.

As I coach people in finance, I often see the same sort of arrogance I had. People get promoted to levels like managing director, portfolio manager, senior vice president, or whatever the next level in their career is, and for some reason, they start to believe they need to know it all.

I remember Charles, a managing director who led a mergers-and-acquisitions team. The team was doing great. He was expanding and adding graduates to his team; they were fresh from the top schools with degrees in all the usual subjects. In other words, Charles was building a team of all-stars who all had the same background as him.

I doubt he would ever admit this, but I think he was a tiny bit intimidated by his direct reports. They operated in a much more casual way than Charles was used to and didn't seem too ruffled by whether he approved of them. Any one of them could have the choice of whatever job they wanted. They knew it, but they chose Charles's team to learn and explore. They were building their résumés. This job could be a stop along the way—or if Charles led them correctly, they could all advance together.

Charles was assigned to work with me as there had been rumblings among these new all-star hires about how he micromanaged them. Their division was profitable and competitive. All eyes were on this team; it probably didn't help

Charles's situation that one of his new hires was the daughter of a board member.

Charles showed up for a meeting with me, looking haggard. I asked what was wrong, and he said that he'd spent the night researching all the critical data points for an upcoming client meeting. Charles wanted to know every minute detail of the deal so if any questions came up from the management team, he could answer.

I couldn't believe it. He had four people working for him, some who were absolute mathematic geniuses. I asked him, "Why didn't you get your team to look at the numbers?" He could've delegated this research work to any of his team members. Charles would have benefited more by asking his team to help than trying to do it all himself and thinking he was the only one capable of the task.

However, because of his need to be "the guy in the know" and not show any perceived weakness, he missed the opportunity to leverage the talents of his team. They all had a fantastic night's sleep before the crucial meeting but were also complaining behind the scenes about not having work that contributed to the broader good of the team. They could have accomplished much more by working together than Charles ever could alone. They would also have been able to play a more active role in the actual meeting by jumping in and helping to answer the client's questions. Instead, they sat in stony silence while Charles ran the show. A leader's job is to let their team's talents soar, not to stifle them by doing everything alone.

Charles would be well served to remember that his team members are just as savvy as he is—if not more so. Working together would put them in a stronger position to strengthen client relationships and remain competitive. The client would see what a powerful, cohesive team they are.

It didn't help that Charles's email communication was also sloppy. Over time he became frustrated, so he had little patience for those around him. He fired off aggressive and ambiguous emails, often with no context. In his effort to excel, he was beginning to decline. When I asked him why he stayed up all night, his answer was "I'm the leader; I need to have a credible level of expertise."

Eventually, Charles saw the light. It took a while, but he started to open up to his team. He told them what he was and was not good at. That humility drove their trust in Charles, and they also started to work together by drawing on the skills the whole team had.

There's no doubt that the best leaders I work with are not only open to feedback and change but welcome it. They don't resist or fight others' opinions, and they don't argue.

Over the coming months, colleagues and other team leaders noticed how Charles's team was more productive, energetic, and engaged.

I see this happen regularly, especially with those used to consistently performing successfully. Embracing the unknown with a bit of gentle humor goes a long way. Sometimes the skills that have served leaders before are no longer benefiting them. I understand this profoundly; all I have to do is think about my run with Laura to remind me. When we are willing to show a little vulnerability, we are in the position to learn the most.

It's true: knowledge is power. We can't be powerful when we are bluffing. We must commit to a continual state of learning. We can only attempt to master anything by admitting there's no possible way to know everything. You don't have to be the expert. You must surround yourself with experts.

Charles must embrace this concept as he hires people. If he employs people who have proficiency and then ties their hands, he'll watch as they exit through a revolving door. It's also important for him to hire a more diverse lineup of employees from different colleges and backgrounds. If you only hear the same stale opinions and thinking, how can you drive creativity and innovation?

Once leaders acknowledge that developing humility in themselves is essential, they can have fun with it. The world becomes a big adventure, and in reality, it is. Sometimes we focus on a narrow target and forget to enjoy our path. Today, especially in finance, we are experiencing extreme change and advancement. Those who are willing to listen, explore, and implement new ideas will win. Encourage your team to liberally share ideas and develop innovative practices, to learn from failed attempts and celebrate creativity. It's okay that your twenty-four-year-old employee knows more about financial modeling than you do. Your goal is to have them come to you as a resource. You want to make sure your team trusts and relies on you as someone they can count on to help them excel.

Your job, and it's a simple one, is to give people the task and allow them to run with it. If you're not accomplishing this, you'll know it by how the team interacts with you and with one another. Morale is a barometer of how well the team is working together.

Once leaders understand the power of humility as a leadership skill, they can develop this awareness in others. If Charles lets go of his need to demonstrate how he can live on three hours of sleep, energy drinks, and strong black coffee, he can develop his team. With the fantastic team he has, the possibilities of what they can accomplish are limitless.

However, if Charles chooses to chase perfection constantly, he is on a sure path to mediocrity. His path to success is clear—he needs to listen and accept that not knowing is not a weakness. That's when accomplishment will begin.

The COVID-19 pandemic forced humility on many of us. The world as we knew it changed drastically in a short time. Activities we unquestionably counted on morphed and were out of our control. We had no choice but to rely on technology to manage meetings and teams. Some did well, while others struggled immensely. Which side did you fall on? What did you do during that time? Did you embrace what was working or quickly forget and force your team back into processes that are now outdated?

A healthy sense of humility will allow individuals to

operate from a position of strength. What we know for sure is that everything can change instantly. Embrace humility while remembering there's always a way to be better next time. Create a culture of feedback with your team. Ensure you receive feedback from the most junior person to the most senior person on your team, and from clients and everyone you interact with. Listen to every opinion possible, because the goal is to continually get better.

Approach every situation as an opportunity to learn something new and to be better than you were before. We can't just understand a concept; we must act to be successful.

ACTION STEPS:

✓ What is your unique expertise? How do you stay on top?

✓ When was the last time you asked for help? Describe it in detail.

✓ Think of your last big mistake. How did you recover? What did you learn?

✓ Think of the last major crisis in your life. What good came from it? What changed forever?

✓ Do you listen before you speak?

✓ Do you ask questions before you make statements?

✓ Do you take time to reflect on the day's activities? How? If not, why not? Would it be possible to isolate and reflect on what you learn daily?

✓ Do you regularly acknowledge all those you work with for their efforts?

✓ Do people come to you and readily share information? Are you micromanaging?

I—INSIGHT

Never stop questioning.

—Albert Einstein (1879–1955)
Theoretical physicist

As leaders progress in their careers, especially technical careers, they can fall into the belief that they will be successful by relying on their academic expertise alone. That's always dangerous—particularly now, when the world is constantly changing and becoming smaller and faster as technology evolves.

There are two critical components to the leadership skill of insight. First, a leader must have insight into themselves, and second, they must have insight into their team. As I discussed in the "A—Action" chapter, I sometimes rely on 360-degree interviews before coaching a client one on one.

These interviews give me insight into how someone operates daily. I want to get a broad perspective from their subordinates, team members, colleagues, and superiors about their strengths and weaknesses.

This is often where I begin to see any "perception gaps." It's not unusual for the people I am working with to say, "No, that's not me" or "No, I'm not like that." They quite often don't have insight into themselves; if they did, they'd be less likely to need coaching. When I share what I've learned through the 360-degree interviews, it's impressive to see how their insight grows, and they begin to change their opinions.

A very talented young woman, Sofia, struggled to motivate her team. She was competent, respected, and a financial wizard. She found that she was the go-to person whenever anyone needed a question answered or assistance in validating the accuracy of financial models. Sofia told me the trouble was that she "had to do everything" herself; nobody would help her. I didn't receive any glaring negative feedback in Sofia's 360-degree interviews. She was well liked and well respected; in fact, people commented how much they loved working with her. I interviewed her, attempting to find the root cause of why she was struggling to get her very talented team to accept tasks and help her. I asked Sofia what she thought the problem was. She replied, "They don't respect me." I shared what I'd learned in the interviews. I quoted phrases I had heard, including "very bright," "good work ethic," "easy to get along with," and "trustworthy." These are wonderful leadership qualities; however, something was still missing. Sofia, too, was perplexed.

I asked her to give me an example. She read me an email she had sent to one of her team members a few days earlier in an attempt to get them to help her. It said:

> If you have time, I need you to build an Excel graph for a presentation I'm giving on Tuesday morning. I'd appreciate it so much. I've attached the raw data for your review. Thank you!

To me, it was clear why Sofia wasn't getting the help she needed—and it had nothing to do with respect. Yet she had no clue what she was doing wrong.

I asked, "Sofia, do you think this is an effective email?"

She replied, "I think so, yes. It's polite, I'm asking for help, not demanding it, and the email is brief. We all get so many emails. I want the assignments to be easy for my team. I even gave this team member the data; all he had to do was verify the assumptions and create a visual."

Helping someone gain insight into their behavior is not as simple as pointing it out. A correction won't work; there must be an awareness shift.

"Sofia, let's break this email down," I suggested. "Your first sentence starts with 'If you have time.' Do you see how that statement could create a problem?"

Sofia paused. "Well . . . everyone works hard and is very busy, so I want to make sure they have time. I also want them to know how much I appreciate their hard work."

Now we had something to work with. I went on. "Sofia, what is the answer to the question 'If you have time?' For example, do *you* have time?"

Sofia laughed. "No, not really . . . I see what you mean."

I continued, "The phrasing of this email allows your team member to reply, 'No, I don't have time,' and by doing so, they have satisfied your requirements. You asked, and the team member answered."

I shared the ACT method with Sofia. Each email needs to include *A*—action, *C*—context, and *T*—timing. By tweaking her process and changing her perception of what a direct request is, thereby leading her to be more direct, she will gain the support of her team. We rewrote it together to be more concrete in the request:

> Good morning,
>
> I need your help putting together an Excel graph for Tuesday morning's 10:00 a.m. meeting.
>
> I've attached the raw data. The data needs to be verified and put into a graph to be inputted into a presentation.
>
> I need it by noon ET on Monday, so I have time to review it.

Please let me know if you cannot make that deadline by Monday 10:00 a.m.

Thanks,

Sofia

Now Sofia's team member has a clear direction. Sofia also has the opportunity to create a contingency plan if the team member cannot get the graph to her by Monday at noon. She added the time designation of ET, so if he's traveling, he'll be aware of her time requirements. If he cannot accomplish the task, there will still be time to develop another solution. By being clear, Sofia is a more decisive leader, and she has enabled her team member to be successful.

When I spoke with her team members as part of the 360-degree interviews, they told me she was overly polite and not direct enough with her communication. It was also cultural; she was British, and her team was all American. Sofia's culture significantly valued a more subtle approach when influencing and engaging people, while her American team members relied on a more direct style to get things done.

Understanding her behavior and how it impacted others is how Sofia gained insight into herself. She also better understood the culture of her team. Some will respond to a direct style; others will want small talk and a personal connection. Sofia is responsible for getting to know her team to understand what each person needs to achieve their own goals and be a strong contributor.

Each member of a team is like a piece of a jigsaw puzzle. It's the leader's job to make sure all the pieces fit together. A leader can build that awareness by knowing the strengths and weaknesses of each team member. The leader should ask themselves a few questions about their team members: What are they good at? In which areas do they need to improve? Sofia needs to spend time with her team to understand them, learning what makes them tick. What motivates them? Where do they want to be in their careers in three years? In ten years? What makes them want to come to work and perform?

Once a leader knows what motivates their team, they can be more effective. Sofia can drive the team toward both their individual goals and broader organizational goals. That's how a leader will impress, get noticed, and get promoted. It's Sofia's job to know where the team is going and help them get there.

The key to gaining insight, as Einstein noted, is to question and to never be satisfied with "good enough." Any situation can be strengthened. It's better to be in the position to question than be blindsided by unwanted behaviors or problems. If Sofia had not taken the time to evaluate why her team member was not performing, several things could have happened. She might have decided leading people was not for her and changed to a more technical career path. But abandoning leadership would have been an unfortunate choice. Sofia was gifted in many ways and had much to contribute. She gave outstanding presentations but could not manage all the details while focusing on delivery. Her team was able to grow because they could "get inside her head." She was now sharing knowledge instead of being the resident expert, allowing her team members to take the next step in their careers.

Insight is a delicate skill. It takes the ability to reflect upon what is going on, what part you play in the dynamic, and what other factors are present. Developing the leadership skill of humility leads right into the advancement of the leadership skill of insight—into yourself, others, and your environment.

I have two stories to share about how I've used personal insight to grow as a leader in my own career. First, as I mentioned earlier, after I exited the military, I completed a postgraduate course in journalism. I wanted to try something completely different and dared to do so even though it was a million miles away from what I had previously been doing. We had a handful of journalists attached to us in Iraq, and it looked like it was exciting and a lot of fun.

When the course finished, my fellow students and I went off to work for local and regional newspapers. Because of the contacts I made in Iraq, I got lucky, and by being pushy, I persuaded the *Daily Express* to assign and sponsor me to cover Beirut, which was an exciting part of the world at that time. I reveled in the action and thrill of being in the middle of world-changing events. I lived in downtown Beirut for several months and traveled all over the region, even to Syria. I also met so many amazing people. Finding out information and making it relevant for a UK audience was exhilarating. But although I had experience in war-torn environments and an education in journalism, it wasn't a good fit. Writing stories just wasn't for me. I didn't enjoy spending my days analyzing sentence structures and selecting the right verb. So I made the tough choice to walk away from it, which I always think is the right choice over sticking with something you know isn't the right fit.

Though journalism wasn't ultimately right for me, I came away with many life lessons from the experience. I think you should always be willing to learn whether an experience will be positive or negative.

Everything we do can be a learning experience if we walk away with a positive attitude. If you don't win a deal, I'll bet you still learn something from losing. Channel that insight and use it next time. We will discuss this more in the chapter on resilience.

Unlike my experience with journalism, Sofia was in the right spot; she just needed to adapt her skills. It's important to know yourself and make decisions that are right for you. Living a life that is not right will make you and everyone around you miserable.

The second story occurred in Iraq and is an example of having insight into others. As we set sail for Iraq, we had to break into two four-person teams. I thought about each team member and then decided who should go into which team. I had one person who could be challenging to work with at times. He was a good guy and incredibly competent, and I liked him, but I had experienced his disruptive behavior first-hand on another deployment. I didn't want him on my team as I knew there would be conflict ahead. There was going to be enough going on without adding the drama of people issues. However, I ultimately chose to take him onto my team for several reasons. First, a new officer was leading the other team. I knew he would be a fantastic team leader in time, but he was new to the unit. I was concerned that it would be a burden if there were conflicts on the team, and I didn't want to place an immediate obstacle in his path. Instead, I put someone very patient on his team to better ensure his success and help him make the right decisions. I made this choice because I had insight into everyone's personalities.

Aspiring leaders need to recognize the importance of their emotions when interacting with people. They need to be aware of what's confusing them and triggering them. Sofia, for example, was taking it personally that her employees were not responding to her requests. Without insight into the situation, she concluded that they "didn't respect her." Nothing could be further from the truth.

This situation isn't unusual; people often jump to conclusions or react without recognizing how their behaviors affect others. Understanding emotions and behaviors is a crucial element in developing the leadership behavior of insight. Understanding what to do with the information helps an individual acquire the leadership quality of emotional intelligence, which is covered in the next chapter. If you have made it this far in the book, you'll find building the leadership skill of emotional intelligence gratifying.

Follow the guidelines listed below to broaden the skill of insight, and remember never to stop *questioning*.

ACTION STEPS:

- ✓ Does your team understand your expectations? How do they know? Have you clearly outlined what you expect of them? If not, why not?
- ✓ How well do you know your team? Do you understand their career goals? Their personal goals? Do you have insight into what motivates them?
- ✓ Do you check in with your team for clarification? Are you confident in your understanding of how people perceive you?

E—EMOTIONAL INTELLIGENCE

You need [IQ], but it doesn't make you a star.
Emotional intelligence can.

—Warren G. Bennis (1925–2014)
American scholar and organizational consultant,
WWII Purple Heart and Bronze Star recipient

U nderstanding and utilizing the power of emotional intelligence (henceforth referred to as EQ) has been the biggest game changer in both my professional and personal life
over the past ten years since I started exploring it in more
detail. I promise that mastering EQ concepts will catapult
your career to new heights. Daniel Goleman, the author of
the comprehensive book *Emotional Intelligence*, is someone
I often refer to as the "godfather of EQ." With his extensive

groundbreaking research, Goleman illustrates that EQ is just as important, if not more important, than IQ (intelligence quotient) when it comes to job success.

IQ, the measure of someone's reasoning ability, or how "smart" they are, is critical in the world where I operate. Executives are moving billions of dollars worldwide and making decisions that affect thousands of people. Consequently, the stakes are high, and leaders need a high level of intelligence, or IQ, to succeed in the world of finance.

As leaders become more senior, however, IQ will only take them so far. Effective relationships are key. The inability to interact with people positively is one of the primary reasons people work with me. Their blind spot in relationship management has halted their career trajectory. Leaders who embrace EQ's power move forward, while those who dismiss it remain stagnant.

Empathy is a core aspect of EQ and is becoming increasingly important in our diverse global economy. In our world of constant connection and continual change, we can no longer afford to think our worldview is the only view. A few weeks into the COVID-19 pandemic, Microsoft commissioned a Harris Poll survey, conducted from May 26 to May 30, 2020. The survey queried 2,285 adults over the age of eighteen and measured employees' empathy for their colleagues. Global employees had experienced considerable shifts in work and home life, requiring many to work at home and some to additionally homeschool their children. Others suffered from illness or were impacted by those who had contracted COVID-19.

The survey asked participants to rank empathy for their colleagues as they managed drastic change. Empathy had gone up worldwide: China ranked the highest, at 91 percent; followed by Mexico, which trailed significantly at 65 percent; the USA scored 61 percent; Italy reported 54 percent; the UK was at 52 percent; and Germany came in last at 50 percent. It's fascinating to review how a shared experience was perceived worldwide. There is no doubt we have never been so empathetic to others because of what we have all experienced. In the early days of remote work during the COVID-19 pandemic, we all had kids and dogs walking into meetings, and it did not bother anyone; we all knew how hard it was to work from home. I hope this new level of empathy continues.

A vice president in an investment bank with about five to eight years of experience will typically spend 80 percent of their time on execution and the technical aspects of their role. As they become more senior, that percentage begins to decline. By the time they make it to the hallowed grounds of the managing director, they are executing less than 50 percent of the time and spending the rest dealing with their team or other external relationships. Having strong EQ is now a crucial skill in the tool kit of every executive. They no longer have the luxury of solely relying on their technical expertise.

Daniel Goleman has argued that IQ will get you the job

but your EQ will determine how quickly you advance and get promoted—and I couldn't agree more. I am often asked whether leadership can be taught and developed or whether it's something you are born with. My opinion is that it's a bit of both. Some people are natural leaders. However, I have yet to meet someone who cannot improve their leadership skills through application and study. My hope is that's why you're reading this book. It might not make you smarter or more intelligent, but if you are willing to be vulnerable and learn something new, *it will improve both your EQ and your leadership skills*. I see it daily, and as I've stated before, it's an absolute game changer.

Over the past few years, I have coached hundreds of executives to develop their EQ, and not one has regretted that investment in time. It is difficult to self-reflect; in fact, I think it is one of the hardest things you can do. However, the journey is worth it, not just for your career prospects and to help build stronger client relationships but also as a human being. I often tell clients that getting a grip on EQ will feel like a weight has been lifted from their shoulders.

The principles Daniel Goleman shared in *Emotional Intelligence*, initially published in 1995, are still relied upon today in business, educational systems, and government organizations. In his book, Goleman discusses the four critical principles of EQ: self-awareness, self-management, social awareness, and emotional awareness.

These concepts are defined as follows:

SELF-AWARENESS

Self-awareness is the foundation of EQ and where we will start this exciting adventure. Developing self-awareness will improve every leadership skill—from listening more and staying calm to asking clients intelligent questions. Without self-awareness, we can't be honest with ourselves or with others. In the last chapter, you started the journey without even knowing it by focusing on insight. Insight is being aware, and intelligence is understanding what to do with that information. I've seen people miss out on a promotion time and time again because they have no idea how their behaviors affect others. If a leader will not attempt to understand the power of EQ, it's only a matter of time before they self-destruct in some area of their life. They may lose their job or a promotion, have a family issue, or experience personal challenges.

A key component of self-awareness is the ability to understand your emotions. Are you aware of emotional triggers that can derail your performance? So many people go through life accomplishing one task after another without giving their day-to-day emotions much thought. We all have our emotions triggered by good and bad events throughout each day, and it's essential to understand and identify them. For example, anger is often thought of as a negative emotion because it can be uncomfortable and disruptive. However, experiencing anger shows that something bigger and more complex is going on with the individual than the situation may warrant.

To help those I'm coaching gain insight into their emotional triggers, I ask them to track such triggers using an EQ diary. It's a straightforward but effective tool, and I strongly suggest you give this a try.

Write down those situations that trigger your emotions throughout the day. Document situations that frustrate or confuse you. Also note which emotions are present when operating at peak performance. By tracking these events and subsequent emotions, you might uncover patterns that will help you avoid being in a frustrating or negative situation in the first place. In addition, you will likely become more aware of potential challenges when emotions begin to surface again, and you might have the tools to avoid letting them derail a situation in the first place. For example, if you realize you get angry while stuck in traffic, adjust your route or timing so you don't leave when the traffic is terrible.

SELF-MANAGEMENT

As awareness of your emotions and triggers grows, striving for emotional balance through self-management will be your next step. Some people mistakenly think they will be successful by denying and suppressing their emotions. The key is to understand your emotions and use them as a tool for greater success.

Other components of self-management include adaptability, an achiever's mindset, and a positive outlook. If a leader cannot adapt, they will remain stagnant and stuck. They'll repeat the same mistakes wherever they go, in different situations. If you are part of the problem, the problem will follow you. An individual with an achiever's mindset will continually look for ways to overcome challenges and solve problems. A positive outlook will help you manage your emotions and avoid wallowing in all that is wrong or could go wrong.

A way to develop self-management is to use the EQ diary to examine the options you could have chosen in any given situation. Look back on something that has triggered you this past week and write out three possible choices you could have made instead.

As discussed in the "C—Communication" chapter, emails are at high risk for misunderstandings and heated interactions. Suppose you received an email and responded to it while you were full of frustration; it may kick off a chain reaction. In email exchanges, there are three options. The first option is to reply quickly without much thought. Option two is to wait fifteen minutes and reflect on your emotions before replying, if there is a chance the email could evoke negative emotion in you or the recipient. The third option is to pick up the phone to discuss the issue. If you decide that answering the email immediately is the right choice, that's fine, as long as you do so strategically and understand the consequences of the decision.

Developing self-management happens through reflection and control. Give it a go this week. ACHIEVERs are constantly seeking the opportunity hidden inside any challenge.

SOCIAL AWARENESS

Social awareness, also known as empathy, is the ability to understand the feelings and perspectives of others. At times you might be surprised that people are offended by your behavior or don't see things the way you do. If this is true for you, I have some good news: *it is possible to cultivate empathy.*

I want to clarify that empathy does not equal weakness, nor does it mean people can walk all over you. On the contrary, strong empathy allows you to make decisions while considering the impact on others—which is a crucial leadership skill.

Some people have a lot of natural empathy. I'm sure you remember the schoolteacher who took more time to explain things to you or the manager who was a mentor to you and went the extra mile to get you involved. These gifted people can read a room and adapt their behavior according to their surroundings. You might hear them say they "sensed something," "felt something," or "noticed something." Those who struggle with empathy will not pick up on things happening right in front of them; instead, they'll plow ahead with their plan and agenda without caring about anyone else. This choice will backfire on them.

Your EQ diary will provide clues as to whether or not empathy comes naturally to you. How often do you find yourself shocked that someone thinks and behaves differently than you expect them to? If someone on your team says, "I felt something," use the questioning skills you learned in the

"I—Insight" chapter to learn more rather than dismissing it as a frivolous statement. Ask, "What makes you say that?" Then listen, *and be careful not to argue with them*. According to our own perspective, we're always one hundred percent right. So take the time to understand *their* perspective. Then discern to the best of your ability what is going on in the situation.

Many leaders are quick to tell me what people on their team can't do well. A common complaint is that team members have poor presentation skills because they are "too quiet" or "go into too much detail." They then tell me how much effort they have put into helping the individual and discussing the practical elements of presenting, including whether the presenter used good eye contact and body language.

I tell these leaders the same thing: you cannot fix the issue until you understand how the person feels before and during the presentation. If a leader asks, "How does presenting make you feel?" they'll get a more complete picture of their team member's emotions. Once they understand how their employee feels, they can demonstrate empathy. For example, the person who shares too much detail might be nervous. If so, the leader can help them overcome their anxiety by suggesting they relax and breathe slowly. They might say something positive before the employee starts their presentation, perhaps by telling them, "You got this!" The leader can connect by sharing how they experienced something similar in their career. Once the relationship and trust are established, the leader can then discuss the practical side of presenting.

I know firsthand that empathy is not something that comes easily to everyone. I am honest enough to admit that I did not demonstrate much empathy during my time in the military.

There was a time in early 2000 when I remember getting notice that space on a combat survival course would be available as soon as I returned from a two-month trip to Bosnia. My girlfriend at the time wasn't as elated at the news as I was. She wanted us to spend more time together since I had just been away for two months. I couldn't see things from her perspective. I was frustrated, thinking, "Why is she getting in the way of my job? Why isn't she as excited as me that I'm going to be running through the woods of southern England for two weeks while being chased by packs of dogs as I desperately try to evade them?" Despite her objections, I went. It was a fantastic course, one of the best I attended—apart from the twenty-four hours of solid interrogation at the end.

As I look back on the situation now, I have no idea how she put up with my behavior and lack of empathy for her for as long as she did. She was the one who had all the empathy. If I had listened, I could have learned a thing or two from her.

If you're like I was back then and don't have much empathy, don't worry—you can improve substantially. But it takes time and patience, and it can be a rough road.

As you embark on the journey of learning, you won't always get it right. Self-reflection on events in which you didn't show empathy can be just as crucial as getting it right in the moment. We all make mistakes. Don't beat yourself up over them. Knowing when you didn't show empathy in a situation is critical and vital to the learning process. You should congratulate yourself when you recognize that you blew it somehow; it shows your self-awareness is growing.

RELATIONSHIP MANAGEMENT

Bringing together the other three aspects of EQ listed above will enable you to build excellent relationships. You'll excel in interactions with both your team and external clients. Working with others requires influence, not direction. People will not robotically respond to commands. Instead, they must understand why they should participate, what's in it for them, and why they should help you succeed.

I recently worked with Peter, a senior member of a midsize asset-management firm who loved to golf. He told me he had issues with team morale and that there had been some complaints about the way he was running the team. Consequently, I was brought in to see if I could help and offer some outside perspective.

During our first conversation, Peter told me his team had just come back from their once-a-month golf day. I asked how it went, and he said, "Fantastic. The team loved it." The truth was *he loved it*, and the team members felt obligated to participate.

"Does the team like the golf days?" I asked, and he went

on to admit there had been a few complaints that not every-one liked golf. After questioning his team, I learned that only three of his eight direct reports had ever picked up a golf club; five team members didn't even play golf.

Peter insisted that golf was "an essential tool for network-ing to succeed in this industry." While he played golf with the team members who enjoyed it, the other five stayed behind and had breakfast while waiting for the others to return. It also turned out that those who didn't play missed out on busi-ness opportunities. Peter often allocated peachy jobs to those who played with him and talked poorly about the others.

Two people on the eight-member team have small kids at home. They told me in 360-degree interviews that they would rather be *anywhere* than on a golf course. In fact, one makes special arrangements with a family member to help get the kids to school on golf days since they start so early. As it turned out, Peter had demonstrated zero empathy for his team by not understanding their situations.

I dug deeper with Peter as I questioned him further about golf day. He realized golf day wasn't a valued team outing; it was all about him and what he wanted. After some gen-tle nudging from me, he spoke to his team members to get honest feedback about golf day. As a result, golf day still goes ahead, but now only every other month—and only those who play golf attend. Those who do attend don't get special treat-ment. Peter conscientiously makes sure work is being dele-gated fairly. In addition, each team member now submits an idea for a team outing. Last month was axe throwing. Peter learned that he excels at throwing axes and is thinking of taking some clients next month.

When I coach someone for whom I know EQ will play a significant role, I try to get them to talk about how they deal with conflict within their team. I find it is an area that can expose how an individual handles EQ. The conversation often reveals the individual's self-awareness. Of course, how they manage conflict is also representative of their self-management. It is a critical area that highlights the importance of EQ—and how much of it someone has. Every perspective must be measured and weighed before drawing any conclusions.

Think about the last time you had a conflict with a team member. What sparked it? How did you feel at the moment? What would you do differently?

Dealing with conflict does not require going head-to-head with someone. Sure, that is occasionally needed, but only when you have complete control of your emotions and have a clear mind. Instead, first think about all the worst-case scenarios. Don't just go into a conflict blind. Do the legwork to make sure you have insight into what the other team member will do. Prepare for every eventuality. What could the person say? How are you going to handle it if they say X? What if they say Y?

In the military the term *fog of war* highlights the uncertainty one experiences during military operations. It's no different when you work on a team. Both on the front line and in a corporate environment, it's important to minimize the unknown.

The next time you experience conflict on your team or with a client, take the time to gather insight and background information. Role-play the discussion in your mind or with a trusted friend. Attempt to look at the situation from the other person's perspective. What questions are they likely to ask? Take a deep breath, park your initial emotions—as they will likely derail the situation—and gather as much information as possible. Once you have a clear picture of the problem, make a calm, strategic decision. That one hour spent gathering information before responding will be the difference between a poor outcome and an effective one. If you need to buy time, tell your client or team member you wish to find out more information before deciding on a course of action.

One common phrase used when discussing EQ is "react versus respond." It means don't react with a knee-jerk response; stay calm. I expand on this phrase and tell those I coach to "not react instinctively but respond strategically."

Hopefully, once your team sees you responding in these situations by staying calm and addressing the problem, they will follow suit. You are coaching and mentoring your team through your actions. You will demonstrate leadership skills they can take with them throughout their career. As they embark upon their own battle to the top, they will undoubtedly encounter a similar situation. And they might remember your leadership and use a similar tactic.

You develop inspirational leadership skills when you learn these skills and implement them with all tasks. Everyone thinks the easiest way to get people to conform is through fear or incentives, but that does not work well. People will resent it. But when people decide to contribute and perform because they want to, you'll have a competitive advantage that will be nearly impossible to destroy.

This book is not meant to be a guide to a healthy and happy household, but the difference strong EQ can make to all aspects of your life, including your home life, is incredible. The people I coach often work long hours and are under enormous pressure. As a result, their home life suffers. This is especially true by the time they work with me, as things have usually reached a boiling point.

I ran a leadership coaching session for a newly promoted managing directors' group at an advisory firm in New York. The group's job was to lead deal teams of junior bankers on mergers-and-acquisitions transactions. This firm is one of the best, so the demands were higher than usual.

On the first day of coaching, I spent the final hour discussing EQ with the group and introducing the concepts of self-awareness and self-management. It is not uncommon to see eyes rolling as I discuss the dreaded word "emotions." I always try to make my coaching as "real world" as possible and stay away from theory. I find this approach resonates with the fast-paced executives in the world in which I operate. I asked them to think of the last time they were pissed off. It didn't take them long, as it is usually due to some email that just came in a couple of hours ago—sound familiar?

I asked them to reflect on it. Who sent it? What emotions came up? Then I asked them to write down how they responded and how quickly. It was not unusual for them to start typing a response to an email that has triggered them before they even got to the bottom of the message. Sound familiar again?

Then I asked them to work through three ways they could have handled the situation differently. We were, of course, going through a real-world EQ diary exercise, even if the participants didn't know it. I saved the activity until late in the day so they could go home and reflect on it.

The following day, as the twelve new managing directors mingled over coffee before continuing the EQ learning journey, one of the participants, Alan, came over to ask whether he could chat with me about something. He told me that although he initially thought about work situations during the previous day's exercise, his thoughts quickly turned toward home. He told me that his wife was always late getting ready and that it inevitably led to conflict, as he would get agitated as time ticked along. He told me it happened again last night, but he was more self-aware. He could feel his trigger happening, but he was a lot more tuned in to his mind and body because of the previous day's session.

So he calmly sat on the sofa as his wife got ready for the dinner date with friends that they had planned. Sure enough, she came into the living room ten minutes late. But this time, he had a massive smile on his face. "You look amazing; let's go when you're ready," he said. She, of course, gave him a quizzical look and asked, "Are you okay?"

The challenging thing about EQ is that you won't always like it. Alan didn't, for sure. He told me he was boiling for those ten minutes on the sofa, but he stayed calm and breathed deeply while he waited. It took a tremendous amount of self-awareness and self-management for him not to walk out into the hallway and yell upstairs. However, the last time he had done that, the journey to the restaurant had been a nightmare. On that occasion, he'd made it even worse by cracking a joke in front of their friends about how his wife was always late and how it made him angry. This time he managed his emotions, which led to a great dinner with his wife.

I often tell those I am coaching that they might not like their newfound self-awareness. It might even bother them not to respond to that email instinctively. But as I've mentioned before, in fifteen years of coaching, I have yet to see an email that can't wait fifteen minutes. When the "fog of war" has dissipated, they will send a vastly different email.

It is not unusual for those who rise through the ranks to never give EQ a moment's thought. In the world of finance, some don't have to, as many people get promoted based on the revenue numbers they pull in and how they interact with certain key members of senior management. But if you don't have EQ, at some point you will hit a wall in your career. And

I see it often with people who are nearing the role of managing director in particular.

One such person was Leonard, who was exceptional in every way—except for his lack of EQ. He had attended an Ivy League university, gone straight to one of the top-tier firms as an analyst, and hit every promotion on time along the way. But as he approached the level of managing director, he found he was struggling.

He'd recently had a meeting with his team where he blew up. Worst of all, it was a recorded Zoom call. It would take Leonard a long time to live down his erratic behavior. You might recall from the chapter on action the "trust bank account" people have with one another. At this point, Leonard was operating at a severe trust deficit. Promotion to managing director was looking like a fading dream, and it was the first time in his life that he had encountered failure. He was not handling it well. Failure was an alien concept to him.

When Leonard and I chatted, he described himself as "tough," and he thought his people were "underperforming" and "not motivated." I had a straightforward and forthright chat with him. I asked Leonard if he had clearly defined expectations for his team. His reply was "They are very well paid and very educated. They should be able to figure it out." Like many leaders, particularly in the well-paid financial-services field, Leonard assumed attractive compensation alone was enough to motivate people. He referred to it often when speaking with them about late nights and long hours.

Leonard had an erroneous view of motivation because he wasn't taking the time to get to know his team. He was holding his people to a standard that he had in his head but had never clearly defined for them. He was so invested in his own career that he didn't know or care about what his employees wanted. He wanted them to be as driven as he was and couldn't understand why they weren't.

After discussing the lack of communication, I shared what I learned from the informal 360-degree interviews. Those who interacted with him said he had "a temper" and could be "demanding." One of the recurring themes from the interviews was "He listens, but not really . . . We end up doing what he wants." Many also stated, "We don't feel valued." The team went on to say that Leonard would drive the agenda in meetings. He would listen to his team develop ideas and then cut them off. One shared, "He didn't even take notes or make eye contact." Leonard would just drive the meeting where he wanted it to go, making the decision he thought was best. Several team members shared with me in confidence that they were planning their exit strategies. Working with Leonard would just be a quick stop along the way in their careers.

The feedback I shared from the 360-degree interviews got Leonard's attention. He was shocked and humbled, now ready to use the EQ diary I had him complete as a tool to help him understand his triggers and his emotional reactions. We reviewed his EQ diary together thoughtfully.

Leonard noted that he tended to become frustrated if someone tried to control the meeting or cut him off midsentence. We took that information and brainstormed solutions. He concluded that one thing he could do was notify the team that there would be a hard stop at the ending time of the meeting. If one team member was going on and on, Leonard could announce, "We've got about fifteen more minutes. I know I haven't covered everything yet, so should we take this offline? If you think it's critical and that we should address it now, then let's do it."

By changing his behavior and providing some instruction, he would allow the employee to participate while enabling the team to manage their time—which most people tend to appreciate. One of Leonard's employees might be an extrovert. Extroverts generally process information by talking concepts through. Introverts, conversely, often need more time to reflect and won't contribute immediately. Leonard might get a thoughtful email with relevant contributions from one of his introverted team members a few days later. It was up to Leonard to learn about his team and which personal attributes contribute to their success. Extroversion is valued in Western cultures but not in all cultures worldwide, which was also something Leonard needed to learn.

As the world becomes smaller, it's essential to remember that certain qualities are not recognized in the same way. Leonard must remember that he needs to hear his team members effectively. He must also check for his own biases.

If the way a team member responds bothers him, but it does not affect productivity, letting it go would be more efficient than talking it out. We need to work with others who are different from ourselves. Otherwise, our work will remain one-dimensional and stagnant. The flip side of the coin is questioning which team members Leonard relates to. If he likes those who follow his direction with limited interaction, why is that the case? Does it feed into his need to feel in control? Or is he getting information that will be valuable to him?

The next task for Leonard was to develop a process to run more-inclusive meetings. It was possible to run efficient meetings while allowing each participant to be heard. Leonard noted that he was not setting agendas for meetings, which needed to change. A quick email or note in a project management tool that included the plan would set the stage for the meeting. Once he distributed the agenda, he could ask the team if anything they would like to address was not on the agenda. If yes, he could add it or address the issue another way. Once the meeting started, Leonard would need to refer to the agenda. If he didn't, the team would observe that the agenda is inconsequential and that the real agenda was *his* agenda.

Leonard still had the unfortunate video documentation of his behavior. There was no way he could deny what he'd done. It doesn't matter how justified he was in his mind; his behavior was crushing. The only way to get over a transgression like the one he had experienced is to acknowledge to the parties involved that it was wrong, move forward, and do better in the future. Leonard's newly found awareness could grow and develop his team. I encouraged him not to worry about the video too much. One unfortunate decision does not erase a positive body of work. Videos are used in professional sports to analyze and review behavior to become a better athlete. I assured Leonard that this video was no different, and he eventually agreed.

Leonard and I sat down and took some time to analyze different situations and how he came across to others. I told him to think about how he would describe someone behaving in the way he had in those meetings. He did not like the way he saw himself. We considered various options he could have taken in those situations, such as not talking as much and listening more, or asking a question of a team member instead of aggressively stating his view. He saw there were other ways of handling his team.

Leonard now does a better job of listening and sometimes even goes along with others' ideas, even when they are not the choices he would have made independently. By taking the time to understand his behaviors and his interactions with others, he was able to realize the value of letting others drive decisions. He recognized that by doing so, he was empowering his team. This is a critical insight, as his team has many employment opportunities elsewhere. If Leonard had remained obtuse, he would have experienced a revolving door of exiting employees. For someone who is fast paced and driven, letting go and giving people a pass can be a very hard thing to do.

Remember, others don't always have your abilities, and they may not do the job to the exacting standards you have; in short, they won't do it how you would have done it. But it is helpful for you to decide what is important and what you can let go of. It's a tricky thing to understand and implement. But by letting go, you will reduce your stress and, at the same time, motivate others. That doesn't mean you are weak or allow sloppy work. Instead, it means you are focusing on the big-ticket items, the things that matter, and you can spend more time with clients and not concentrate on something small—like the font being the correct size on a report.

Developing EQ is challenging, and there are no short-cuts. Some will implement self-management, self-awareness, social awareness, and relationship management, but only on the surface. They may state they care about developing their teams, but only when they think they are being observed. They may become aware of their emotions but turn around and suppress them. This in turn may lead them to create other counterproductive activities, such as working too many hours or other bad habits. An EQ charade won't last for long. Embracing EQ creates lasting transformation in leaders and their organizations.

If you need help in this area, surround yourself with people with high EQ and listen to them. Question yourself when you think that you are right and there are no other options.

There is always something to learn. Allow your team to manage their emotional health so they, too, can develop EQ. Set a goal to strive for team EQ, and practice these skills together.

Once leaders begin to develop EQ, they will become coaches and mentors. Nothing gave me a bigger thrill than seeing one of my old team members leave the unit because they were promoted or moved on to better things. I was put on the maritime counterterrorism team, whose role is to protect ships and oil rigs off the UK coast. The task falls to the elite Special Boat Service, and we were attached to them for a few months. One member of our team had just passed Special Forces selection and was now in the Special Boat Service. I remember visiting the base in Poole on the southern coast of England, and as I walked through camp, I bumped into him. I was so proud of what he had achieved. I think he was a little taken aback by my over-the-top praise. But he came from our unit, and I was so happy for him to get through the brutal selection process.

I have always taken great pride in the achievements of others; I think it's one of the reasons I enjoy coaching so much. I feel the same way when someone I'm coaching in financial services "gets EQ." Once I observe their perceptions and behaviors changing, I know they are on the path to building a rewarding and impactful career.

Do you see the success of others as your own success? If you don't, that might be something you need to address.

I recently had a catch-up call with someone I had coached.

Our coaching engagement had ended months before, but we stayed in touch. Just because I'm no longer working with a client doesn't mean I don't care about what happens next for them. I try to keep up with as many former clients as possible. While we talked, his daughter came into the room and asked to whom he was speaking. He said to his coach. His daughter then came on the line and thanked me for my work with her father. He was calmer at work but also at home. He had gone through a fantastic EQ transformation, and it was now permeating every aspect of his life. It was one of the most memorable moments in my coaching career. He still got it wrong from time to time; we all do. It's important to recognize when you get it wrong as it's a sure sign your self-awareness is growing. Just make sure you learn from it and try to get it right the next time a similar situation arises.

Whenever the opportunity arises to develop EQ, you should seize on it, as it is such a vital life skill. You can have a major effect on your team if you take a breath and apply the principles in this chapter. Those who embrace EQ's importance will lead happier lives filled with profound experiences and prosperous relationships. Every aspect of EQ plays a role and can be used to discuss the development of the leadership skills of strong leaders.

ACTION STEPS:

✓ Start your EQ diary.

✓ Build a plan to strengthen the four elements of EQ: self-awareness, self-management, social awareness, and relationship management.

✓ Research and read about the topic. Here are a few great books to consider reading:

- *Emotional Intelligence* by Daniel Goleman, 1995.
- *Emotional Intelligence 2.0* by Travis Bradberry and Jean Greaves, 2009.
- *Emotional Agility* by Susan David and Christina Congleton, 2016.

V—VISION

Good leaders set vision, missions, and goals
. . . When everyone is united in purpose . . .
you have a winning team.[1]

—General Colin L. Powell (1937–2021)
Former US secretary of state and
chairman of the Joint Chiefs of Staff

I n workshops and coaching sessions, I find myself telling participants lacking vision that they are merely putting out fires all day, which to me seems like a dreary existence. Executing tasks not grounded in a vision will not leave a mark on the world, and it certainly won't create a legacy.

Creating a vision, clearly outlining where you're trying

---

1. Colin Powell, *It Worked for Me: In Life and Leadership* (New York: HarperCollins, 2012).

to go, is something the military does well; it's ingrained in us. Military personnel understand the vision of their commander, their mission, and their role in it, whether they are asked to kick down a door or take a hill. The person in charge will continually share their vision at the start of the day and constantly throughout the mission. The vision is usually pretty simple, not because those on the team aren't smart, but because enough is going on without complicating things.

To help those I coach grasp the concept of vision in their day-to-day lives, I developed the acronym ARC, which stands for *aspirational, realistic,* and *clear.*

> **Aspirational**—Where are you going? You might not know how you're going to get there yet, but at least you have an idea of what you're ultimately trying to achieve. By outlining this aspirational aim, you are giving yourself a focal point for what you hope your future will look like, whether that is in two days or two years.

> **Realistic**—Your vision must be grounded. Everyone wants to be the best, the fastest, and the most profitable. But be realistic in your vision, or you will quickly lose your followers. This is the time to build your plan on how you intend to get to your vision. Your aspirational aim may change as you reflect on

how realistic it is in the time frame you have. Chop up the time and attack the vision piece by piece. Maybe that means a step-by-step chronological time frame.

Clear—Communicating clearly is essential if you want your team to follow and join your vision. It is not enough to define a vision; you also must create buy-in from your team and your stakeholders to execute it. You will only get that through a clear and straight-forward message. Define a clear, compelling leadership vision that everyone can willingly support. The vision must be simple; there's enough complexity going on in the world already, especially in the fast-paced world of finance.

Continuously demonstrate your commitment to your vision by reminding your team of it, both individually and in meetings. Share what you believe in as the leader. When leaders provide a vision to their teams, it fuels confidence and inspires teams to succeed. If you don't know where you want to go, your team will have zero chance. If leaders don't explain the purpose of the vision, their followers won't get it. They won't connect to the goal, and they won't care whether the mission is accomplished. Understand what makes your team different from any other team. Why should someone want to work with your team over another?

President John F. Kennedy shared an impressive vision as he addressed Congress on May 25, 1961. He stated that the United States "should commit itself to achieving the goal, before this decade is out, of landing a man on the moon and returning him safely back to the Earth." The vision was achieved just eight years later, on July 29, 1969.

Every person working on the space program at that time knew why they were doing what they were doing. Whether they were working on advanced mathematics to help plan the mission's route or cleaning out the bathrooms, everyone understood they had a role to play, which undoubtedly gave them drive and pride. There's a story that has become famous folklore about a janitor sweeping the floor at NASA. An executive asked him what he was doing. The janitor replied, "I'm helping to put a man on the moon."

When I was on my unit, we often worked with people from other military arms—engineers and artillery, for example. I'd always ask everyone I met what they were doing and why they were doing it. If they didn't know or had a vague answer, it was a quick assessment that the leader had a problem. I still use this tactic when I'm coaching leaders in financial services. If a clear statement of why every team member is there and how they contribute to the bigger picture does not emerge, I know there is a problem. Like the man sweeping the floor, everyone should clearly understand how they fit in.

Don't be afraid to ask your team members how they see their contribution fitting into the company's overall mission. Their answers will be very telling, and it only takes a minute. We don't have to look too far to find present-day examples of vision. Elon Musk, CEO of Tesla, was certainly a visionary in 2008 when he announced affordable electric vehicles in the future. While many companies and individuals battled the recession of 2008, Musk was visualizing a future many had not even dreamed possible. He was criticized at the time as Tesla was nearly broke. It seemed impossible they could achieve this aspirational goal. Still, he followed ARC: he had a clearly laid out, aspirational, realistic plan that could be achieved, and he communicated it clearly. Just five years after Musk's original announcement—and after a devastating recession, no less—Tesla's Model 3 was born at a price tag of $35,000. And Tesla continues to move forward in designing even more-affordable electric vehicles. That's because Musk has a clear vision and makes sure everyone in his company is driving toward it.

Flash forward to 2021, and watch Musk's vision of creating electric cars continue to expand. Mary Barra, CEO of General Motors (GM), proclaimed GM would have a fleet of electric vehicles by 2035. When Barra and the leadership team announced this vision, applications started pouring in. This was especially noteworthy in 2021, as companies struggled to recruit and retain employees during the Great Resignation. Employees were demanding flexibility and alternative pay

scales. Having a clear vision changes the recruiting game; potential employees will flock to participate in something that
they deem bigger than themselves. Work is no longer a grind
but an exciting place to be.

Barra reported that she started receiving thank-you notes
from employees who were grateful to be part of shaping the
future of a company they believed in. Although the details
weren't exactly clear on *how* GM was going to get there, employees were engaged in the vision and confident that they
would play a role in bringing it to life. When one person
achieves what was once thought impossible, the idea gains
momentum.

Barra did not get into the details because she trusted
those who worked for her. She knew that with a clear vision
and intelligent, motivated people under her, the job would get
done. So think of where you want your team to be in twelve or
twenty-four months, and see if they can come up with innovative and exciting ideas to get there. Sometimes the aspirational part alone is enough to get the team moving, and they
will help you plan and find a way to get there.

Empowering your team is a compelling motivator.

If you have a clear vision, there is no way you can lose,
and it's not necessary to be the president of the United
States, Elon Musk, or Mary Barra to do it. Any employee, at
any level, can utilize the power of vision. I see examples in
my coaching practice all the time.

Sandra, a leader at one of the major Canadian banks whom

I was working with, shared that her team of thirty bankers didn't seem motivated no matter what she did. She explained that the group was plodding along, achieving their daily tasks but not going above and beyond. She explained that their work was satisfactory but not stellar. She was concerned they were doing the minimum to get by. I asked Sandra what direction she gave them, and she replied, "What do you mean?" I was beginning to identify the root cause of the problem. The team did not have direction; there wasn't much to get excited about. They were doing the daily grind, with no creativity or innovation in their work.

I asked her where her group ranked compared to their peers at other large Canadian banks. Sandra responded that they were currently ranked fifth in terms of deals completed over the last year. "Where do you want to be," I asked her, "and when do you think you can get there?" Sandra was now furrowing her brow, clearly confused, almost puzzled by the question. It turned out she was fine with the ranking of fifth.

Now I was aware of the information and skills that Sandra needed to be successful. I told her that the team's mediocre, stale attitude stemmed directly from the top, and the buck stopped with her. She was visibly taken aback by my direct approach. I doubt anyone had spoken to her in such a forthright manner in a long time. Sandra was now starting to get it. When I asked her again, "Where do you want to be?" she changed her answer to "We'd like to be number one!"

At this point, I introduced Sandra to the concept of ARC.

Rising from fifth place to first was aspirational, but it was not realistic—not in the near future, anyway. She was dealing with an unmotivated team; they did not have an infrastructure to help them progress. A positive slogan such as "We'll be number one!" isn't enough to move the team forward. Luckily Sandra was coachable and continued to work with the ARC concept. After reflecting on my pushback that number one might be a bridge too far, she agreed and became more realistic. She took it step by step and built a plan with the senior members of her team. She returned to me and shared, "I'd like my team to aim to be number three in Canada within the next two years." Even I was motivated by this statement. I could envision her team of thirty bankers starting to become engaged in this goal. I see it happen all the time. When a leader makes a shift and takes action, it's enriching for me as a coach. She had mapped out the next two years quarter by quarter and could see rising two places in that time as an aspirational and realistic goal. ARC was working for her. Now she needed to communicate it clearly to the team.

Once Sandra had a realistic goal as part of her vision, she began to outline the practical steps she would take to get there. A communications plan emerged from her process. She noted that there would need to be improvements in the information technology (IT) process and asked her team to bring ideas to improve it. Sandra would need support from her team to speak to the IT department to determine whether there were any systems available to help with planning and tracking progress. The ways the team pitched to clients and told their stories were measured by whether or not the communication would help them get to number three within two years. This simple vision created cross-functional engagement, which is crucial for successful banks.

As the momentum continued, Sandra laid out a clear road map for her team and other departments to follow. But not everyone needed to know the whole two-year plan at once. Some of them only got the next six months, which they needed to move the needle in their role. Sandra's deputy got the whole picture, and this was essential as they had to help the team focus when required. Another element in a communications plan is to determine who needs to know what and when.

Employees began collaborating and sharing ideas. Sandra had lit a torch under the team! The new shared ambition drove many of them to produce more than they had before. But, of course, not everyone grasped the vision. It wouldn't be realistic to think they would. Some couldn't handle the ambition and new pace and decided to leave the team. The people who left weren't connected to the vision. That's okay; it's much better that they realize they are not a good fit than for you to endure their mediocre contributions.

To keep her team focused, Sandra frequently asked them in meetings, "Is this going to get us to number three?" Her team started to expect the question; they were then more strategic in their planning and were ready for the question and began to answer it themselves.

Two years later, Sandra's team *ranked number two* in
their category. She exceeded her goal of becoming number three. Now employees were trying to get transferred to
Sandra's team. Her direct reports were promoted because of
their increased performance.

Some leaders are tempted to create stretch goals that are
not attainable. But without the realistic component of ARC,
stretch goals become defeating. In the direst circumstances,
people will cut corners to achieve the vision. Sandra did not
have to create a stretch goal—by laying out clear expectations,
her team accomplished more than they aspired to. This is
very common; there is no need to push harder than necessary. When I last talked to her, Sandra shared that she is now
focusing on being number one. I have no doubt she will lead
her team there. She understands the tools of ARC and vision
and uses them well.

Michael, a banker I was coaching, knew he had a slight
chance of winning a new client. He only got the meeting as
a favor, as his kids went to school with one of the company's
private equity owners. Six banks were competing for the
same deal, and he was the rank outsider, with no previous
experience with the client. We discussed the ARC approach,
and Michael decided to take a risk and use it to shake up his
pitch process. His aspiration was, of course, to win the deal
on his own, but realistically he knew he would likely need to
share the deal with one of the other banks. He rolled the dice
and tried a novel approach.

Instead of creating nonstop pie charts and using bullet points to tell the story, which is the traditional way, Michael produced a pitch book that looked vastly different from his bank's standard template. He included fresh images of the client with clean titles that spoke only about how he could help them get the deal they wanted. The client was constantly featured throughout, and it was all about them. He included bullet-point stories of everything the company would achieve by selecting his bank's services. He spoke of the deals in which he had worked alongside other banks. It was a memorable presentation that people talked about for a long time. No one gave him the direction to be creative; Michael just ran with the idea. I thought what he designed was brilliant. Risk is part of creating a plan and a vision. Michael imagined the possibility of doing something different. Since six banks were competing for the client's business, he took the gamble to attempt to stand out—and it worked.

In the military, we rehearsed situations to determine whether any unforeseen challenges would arise; then we'd build a plan to mitigate them. As you draft your plans and vision, ask yourself what challenges might prevent you and your team from reaching your goals. Thoughtfully managing risk is the only way to create big wins. Be prepared to be overwhelmed by the team's success and accomplishments when they are grounded in a clear vision.

If you are a team member and are not aware of your team's vision, don't be afraid to ask what it is. Suppose you are in the position to lead your team; design a vision. As I've shared before, mentoring and coaching a team, instead of simply managing tasks, is when leadership becomes fun. Teams will achieve more than you ever envisioned possible. Like the great leader General Colin Powell, I believe that compelling visions can create better teams and even a better world.

Follow the guidelines listed below to do your part in creating a vision, building stronger teams, and, yes, influencing a better world.

ACTION STEPS:

✓ What leaders inspire you and why? What vision do they share? Is there a way you can emulate it?

✓ What can you do to influence a vision as part of a team? Are you just completing tasks, or are you helping to achieve something far greater?

✓ If you are leading a team, start designing a vision using ARC. Make sure that it is aspirational enough to engage people. Don't forget to be realistic in your expectations. Resist the temptation to create unattainable stretch goals. Be clear in all your communications.

E—EXECUTION

Leadership is the ability to get people to do
what they don't want to do and like it.

—Harry Truman (1884–1972)
Thirty-third president of the United States

E xecution is all about one thing: getting the job done. It's why the realistic element of ARC (aspirational, realistic, and clear) in the "V—Vision" chapter is so important. Vision will only take you so far; we've all worked with people full of imagination and good ideas who don't know how to get the job done. When the people I coach propose a solution that is a little out there, I often suggest that they might be joining the "good ideas club." Without solid execution, even the most brilliant ideas will fall flat. Execution comprises learning to motivate, delegate, and give/receive feedback, all of which are essential to becoming an ACHIEVER and succeeding in the battle to the top.

When entering the workforce or a new company, everyone starts at ground zero. It may not seem fair, but you must prove yourself, once again, to advance in your career. If you seek a promotion, you will have to go after it; it won't come to you. You must execute successfully.

One key factor that can enable you to execute successfully is to understand and adapt to the corporate culture. You'll begin to recognize unique customs and traditions by listening and observing. Another clue is corporate folklore. What stories are told? Who are the heroes, and who are the villains? Stories provide great insights into why people do the things they do to achieve goals.

Some organizations might be very collegial, meaning there's much socialization. Others might be highly collaborative, where every person gets a say before a decision is made. Some might value being autonomous, where the expectation is that the professional is individually accountable for completing tasks. It's a big mistake to barrel through a company or department without understanding why and how people do things the way they do. You might have heard that employees don't quit because they dislike their company; they leave because they are not getting along with their manager. From my experience, this is true.

One thing that can hinder your ability to execute is not

believing in the abilities of those around you, especially the younger generation. When you were in graduate school, I bet getting that dream job in finance seemed like mission impossible. As a result, you may now expect everyone to work as hard and be as motivated as you were. Unfortunately, that's not how the world works.

In our initial meetings, I hear from countless executives that the younger generation "doesn't get why they have to push themselves" and "won't work long hours." Then they complain about all they did to earn their promotion. Thinking you are the hardest-working person in the room is pretty common. I'll hear a steady stream of complaints from the new managing director about how they "can't find good talent" and how much harder they worked when they were associates. They'll tell me how easy this new generation has it, using smartphones, good internet service, and advanced computers.

As I listen to their recital of discontent, I realize I've been guilty of this perception myself. When I finished Commando training in 1999, I thought I had it way harder than anyone who had done the course before. The truth is it's just as hard today as it was in 1999 and as it was in 1940. However, when you are the one who is going through the grueling training, it seems like it's never been more challenging. We are so mired in our own experiences and opinions that it's often difficult to empathize with anyone else. Upon further reflection on my time in the military, the most challenging aspect wasn't jumping out of planes or doing any number of dangerous things; it was managing people and getting them to do what needed to be done. I bet it's the same for you.

No one can achieve all that is possible in a leadership role while working alone—nor are they expected to. In contrast, those who can grasp the concepts of motivation, delegation, and the power of giving and receiving feedback are at the top of their game. Senior leaders will notice the effectiveness of these savvy leaders. They want to be around them and will enthusiastically welcome them into the senior ranks of their organization.

The following sections break down elements of motivation, delegation, and feedback so you can learn to use these skills yourself.

MOTIVATION

Motivation is complex because no two people are the same. Without understanding what motivates the individuals on your team, you will face an uphill battle to get anyone to do anything. One great way to find out what motivates people is to ask them who they feel was their best manager and why. I do it all the time when I first meet someone I'm getting ready to coach. You'll hear stories about times when a manager trusted them, gave them meaningful tasks, or allowed them to work autonomously.

Missing the potential to maximize a talented team will

stifle a leader's career. As you progress up the promotion ladder, the workload will increase. I've observed that the most challenging hill in the battle to the top is in the vice president's role: those middle years where the workload increases incredibly. Leaders who fail to learn how to delegate or motivate their team will end up doing all the new work on top of their old responsibilities and will burn out. The exhausted employees either remain stagnant in their jobs or leave finance altogether.

To thrive in the workplace, it's crucial to understand what motivates *all those you interact with*—junior team members, senior managers, and peers. You must make it your mission to understand your team's unique drivers and what makes each member tick. Not every task is glamorous; many of them are not. Ask your most junior team member if they enjoy changing the fonts and color schemes on your decks for evidence of that.

A few years ago, I was working with the head of investment banking at one of the largest banks in the world. During a conversation about the art of motivation, this wise leader noted that everyone on his team was "either learning or earning," and he deduced that an employee was very likely planning their exit strategy if neither was happening. As a result of understanding his team's motivations, he attracted and retained the most coveted talent.

Academic research on the topic of individual motivation is abundant, and it is all valid. But let's first deal with the elephant in the financial-services room—*many people are motivated by the significant earning potential of a financial-services career.* This truth might surprise you, because research suggests that money is not the only motivator. Instead, the pundits indicate that intrinsic motivators such as personal challenge, enjoying the work environment, or just plain old curiosity motivate people to perform.

I agree with their findings; however, from my years of experience coaching those in financial services, earning a significant income is, to a certain degree, also a strong motivator. The reality is that financial services and other high-earning jobs are unique, and generalized research does not apply. Many leaders start out thinking money is their team's core motivator, but I've witnessed situations where money starts to become a demotivator. Understanding perceptions and misperceptions will help you to maximize the potential of your highly compensated, talented team.

Barry was an aspiring portfolio manager in a large asset-management company based in Chicago. He had risen through the ranks in a typical fashion without any noticeable bumps in the road, but now he needed a little help. Barry was a specialist in researching and investing in Midwest industrial firms and was now on the path to running his own fund inside the firm. However, when I first met him, it didn't take him long to bring up money. He felt underpaid compared to his peers and spent most of our first chat telling me how frustrated about it he was.

I asked Barry how he knew he was underpaid. He said that while he didn't know what his peers earned, he knew he was not paid enough. So I dug deeper to find out why it frustrated him so much, since he made a salary that provided a very satisfying life. He replied, "I don't feel valued; I just want to be paid what I'm worth to the firm." This was a classic example of money being a demotivator. To the average person on the street, his income would be life changing; however, Barry viewed it as a marker of his value to the firm. He didn't need the extra cash. He already had the house, the car, the vacations. Of course, more is always nice, but at what point does it stop motivating and become a mark of your value?

The Three Elements of Money Motivation

Money must have three essential elements to avoid the risk of demotivating employees. First, it must be fair. In Barry's situation, he felt he was undercompensated compared to his peers relative to the work he did. He also perceived that his earnings did not reflect his effort. Second, there needs to be openness. Barry had no idea what others were earning, and I'm not suggesting he needs to know. Management should be transparent about how the system works. Explain how the individual's bonus or salary fits into the bigger picture. Thinking salaries are secret is an unfortunate myth. People talk, and there are online databases that record salaries.

The third element of financial motivation is parity, where those working in a similar space know they are all within the same approximate area. If a member of your team is underpaid, consider having the courage to correct the disparity. Another competitive firm will quickly snatch them away if you choose not to. Many firms spend a ton of money recruiting talent with signing bonuses, stock options, and other perks. Unfortunately, that process falls flat when retaining talent. I'm not suggesting paying people more just to keep them, but I am suggesting that leaders can proactively correct disparities.

Using these three essential elements—fairness, openness, and parity—will help you navigate the annual bonus-season conversation with more insight. Furthermore, if you commit to considering all three, you will avoid ending up with team members as unsatisfied as Barry.

The problem with paying people more without understanding the underlying motivations is that it won't take them long to acclimate to the new money. So in my experience, trying to retain people with money alone rarely lasts. The employee will leave within six months anyway. Understanding *why* the employee wants more money will create a stronger partnership and an enviable team.

What could the asset-management firm have done to let Barry know he was valued? They might promote him early by giving him some recognition and allowing him to create and run his own fund. They might acknowledge him publicly in the media or internally at the company. They can explain how they calculate his bonus and how it's dependent on various factors, so he sees it as fair. There are countless ways to recognize his contribution without immediately ponying up more money. This practice is critical because there may not always be access to funds when trying to remain competitive in the financial-services marketplace.

I've seen it time and time again: leaders shying away from conversations with their employees about money because they don't have as much influence as they'd like to be able to increase salaries. However, that is not a reason to avoid the conversation. Instead, understanding the three elements of money motivation and discussing them will reveal what a leader *can* do to retain their key talent. The open dialogue will also build trust with the team, creating agility in decision-making and execution.

People who gravitate toward financial services are driven and focused, but they also like to develop and learn. If they don't see the opportunity to be intellectually creative in their role, they quickly lose focus. When younger employees join the firm and you invest time to develop them, they stay. Even if they leave, they have nothing but good things to say about you and the organization.

There's a danger in becoming too comfortable doing things the way they have always been done. The American sociologist Diane Vaughan coined the term "normalization of deviance," describing how the departure from proper behavior becomes normalized in corporate culture.[2] Her original example was the events leading up to the space shuttle *Challenger* disaster in 1986, where many unchallenged mistakes happened along the way.

Before the pandemic in 2020, I worked with an aspiring fund manager, Kyle, who wanted to inject more technology into the team's stock-picking process. Douglas, the senior manager, resisted any change. He saw no reason to change what had been functioning without fail. Kyle was so frustrated that he couldn't influence or question any existing processes that he told me he was thinking about leaving. When I discussed this with Douglas, he was shocked. I advised him to have an open mind and see what could be developed by using new technology—and fortunately, he agreed. Douglas listened and supported the new technological integration, ultimately discovering that his current system could improve its process and capability. Kyle stayed, and it had nothing to do with money. He is now in a prime position to take over running the fund at some point in the near future.

Motivating employees to stay on the job isn't always the end goal. One firm I work with actually encourages its associates to leave within two to three years. The firm knows they can't promote them all, and if they did, they would be top-heavy with talent. So instead, they treat the associates incredibly well during these two to three foundational years. As a

---

2. Diane Vaughan, "The Challenger Launch Decision," (1996) https://pubmed.ncbi.nlm.nih.gov/25742063/ accessed 2/3/2022.

result, when the young executives tell stories of their previous employer, the company wins by attracting more business and new talent based on their reputation.

Learning is not just putting people through rigorous training courses. Your employees should also learn from you. Take time to develop your team and show them how to do things you learned through your experience. In other words, give them something that no course can—*your time.*

I've said it before—this is where leadership becomes fun. You won't only be achieving goals and tasks; you'll be impacting people's lives. I'm sure you know how organizations change when respected CEOs or senior leaders leave. We miss their presence because they gave of themselves.

We can share our unique imprint wherever we go. If you're not dispensing your wisdom and insights, all the hard work in leading and motivating a team becomes meaningless. In the chapter on action, I discussed how much General Sir Peter de la Billière, influenced my career and my decision to join the military. *You* have the potential to be that leader for someone else. And you might even become the leader people mention when a coach asks them to describe the best manager they ever had.

DELEGATION

To properly delegate, it is essential to understand and accept that your team will not perform any task the way you would.

When describing what you want your team member to do, remember the acronym ACT—action, context, timing—that we discussed in the "C—Communication" chapter. This tactic also works fantastically well for delegation. Describe what *action* you want them to do, the *context* and why you want them to do it, and the *timing* of when you need the action completed. Employees are not machines that mindlessly execute. Ensure you engage anyone you delegate to in the overall vision, regardless of the tasks they perform. Remember, it's a great idea to articulate your vision before starting a meeting or kicking off an initiative. If your actions don't match your words, you'll break the bond of trust with your team members.

As you learn to delegate, you'll start achieving more than you thought possible as you tap into the talent and potential of your direct reports. You'll benefit from new ideas and learning new ways of doing things. Finally, you'll learn to accept that something doesn't have to be perfect by your standards to be functional.

Jane, a vice president at a large bank based in New York, was struggling to delegate to her associate, who had recently joined the team straight from an MBA program. Jane's team was running a cross-border deal with a company based in Mexico City, and Jane was dealing with everything, including tasks that should have been delegated to her associate. The problem was that Jane just couldn't let go. The associate was becoming increasingly frustrated, as he felt he offered no value to the team. Eventually, he complained to the managing director, who called me in to help.

It didn't take long for Jane to realize she was holding on to too much. The good news was that she was brilliant, and with a bit of an outside push, she managed to let go of the work she should have delegated down, which freed up her time to look at the more strategic parts of the deal. "Getting out of the way" can be challenging; if she wasn't doing the work, how could Jane show the value she brought to the team? But her value wasn't doing her old job on top of her current responsibilities. She was also crushing the ambition of her associate, who undoubtedly had talent. She also discovered her associate had spent a summer working in Mexico City and could chat with their team about nonbanking matters; they even knew the same restaurants! You just never know what skills someone brings to the table unless you ask and get out of the way.

Sometimes we don't delegate to other people because we assume they don't have anything to offer. For example, when I was in Kuwait waiting to go into Iraq, we had an old marine called Terry who worked in logistics and had never been promoted. He loved what he did; he was passionate about logistics and being a marine. Moving up is not for everyone; Terry was happy where he was. He didn't have much to do in Kuwait at this point, during the buildup to war, so Terry decided to erect a tea tent where anyone was welcome to stop in, grab a cup of tea, and chat. I dropped in one day and learned

Terry had been in the first Iraq War. I asked whether he had any tips for me, such as bits of kit that worked or didn't work. To my surprise, Terry came alive. He enthusiastically shared all he knew. He had terrific insights into the gear we used and what to take and not to take. Terry knew what he loved to do and was happy. When you're leading a team, it's essential to know your team members' motivations. Despite Terry's rank, he was a vital asset.

Effective delegation is not only about communicating the end goal to your team, but it can also include how you expect them to behave, especially if it's something new to them. I had an experience while coaching a chief technology officer called Mark. He introduced to his team a project management chat system to facilitate communication. Unfortunately, two of his direct reports working on a task he had assigned were openly arguing in the chat about completing the work. One accused the other of slacking off, and the other reported that the accuser was unskilled. It was a nightmare, as everyone on the team witnessed the argument. Mark let it go for a while, as he hoped they would sort it out as adults, but they didn't. He then requested a meeting with them to provide feedback on their behavior. One took the feedback well, but the other didn't, as he couldn't understand why it was a problem.

I'd asked Mark if he'd ever explained the system and how it should be used for his direct reports. He seemed surprised at the question, replying, "It's a chat system. They should know what it's for." "True," I said. "But do people understand what kinds of behaviors are and are not appropriate in the system?" He had to admit he hadn't laid out his expectations about what types of conversations were acceptable. His direct reports were recent college graduates who had never known life without technology; in fact, one of them had joined during the pandemic and had never set foot in an office before. So from their perspectives, they were not doing anything wrong. They had no idea arguing this way in a work forum was inappropriate until Mark told them. Their only experience of using similar functionality was through social media, where we all know arguments occur frequently.

Generation Z and many millennials have never known a world without technology. They've had instant access and are used to reaching out to their online communities to find answers. They want fulfilling careers and meaningful work. They'll be quick to leave a job that is not helping them realize their goals. Any leader who fails to understand these generations' motivations will have a constant revolving door of employees.

And when you're working with older generations, show respect regardless of their status or title. They've paid dues you haven't paid and have had experiences you'll never fully understand. Just as I was able to gain invaluable insights from Terry in his tea tent, you will have a wealth of wisdom to rely on if you take the time to seek to understand. The insights you gain will become a distinct competitive advantage.

GIVING AND RECEIVING FEEDBACK

Feedback in the military is constant. From the day you arrive at the Naval College to begin officer training, you get feedback on how you're doing, both positive and negative. The same feedback culture does not exist in the corporate world, not in my experience. I have yet to see a team in the finance world that gives and receives feedback the same way. And that is a shame, because I think most teams can improve with it.

How do we cultivate a continuous culture of feedback? First, as the leader, make sure you are taking feedback well. That means listening to it and not reacting instinctively if you disagree with it. You will remember that in the EQ chapter, we discussed managing emotions. You have a fantastic opportunity to do just that when you receive feedback. Absorb what is being said, be attentive, and show you are listening. Then take it away and digest it; let it percolate for twenty-four hours. Then, and only then, react to it. It may not always be appropriate, but sometimes you should thank the person who gave it to you. It takes a certain amount of courage to provide feedback, especially to someone more senior, so respect that and show you appreciate and have acknowledged it.

When I'm coaching large groups of people, I'll ask, "How many of you would like more feedback?" I'll typically see around 90 percent of the people in the room raise their hands. I'll then ask, "How many of you have given feedback to anyone in the last two weeks?" Then I usually see about 10 percent raise their hands to answer this question.

One of the areas I especially see lacking is giving feedback to high performers. Think of that one person on your team, the one you rely on most, the one you go to with all your problems. How often do you give them feedback? Since they are consistently and successfully executing, they are often ignored when it comes to feedback. The irony is that they need more input than others—they have a thirst for it. The best athletes in the world, in every sport, get to the top by receiving and then acting on feedback to improve their skills. Giving feedback is only one side of the coin; be sure to ask for feedback as well. Top athletes certainly do.

A human resources executive for the wealth management division of one of the world's largest banks told me their junior members were leaving in unprecedented numbers. When I asked why, she said, "The biggest thing they are telling us is they are fed up doing jobs and not being told why they're doing them."

I took the comment seriously. I wanted to uncover for myself the cause of what was becoming known as the Great Resignation. During a leadership course at a similarly sized bank a few weeks later, I asked the group of newly promoted directors I was coaching, "Are you giving time and guidance to your team?" The answer was universal: no, they were not. They told me it was for two reasons: first, they are just too busy, and second, why should they? Their junior team members are leaving in droves, so why invest the time in someone they sus-pect will go anyway? This perpetual circle was causing scores of young achievers to leave. Someone must stop this cycle of destruction, and my argument to the directors was that they needed to be the ones to do it. I told them to remember what it was like to be grinding away until the early hours on a task you had no insight on; it's soul-destroying. Use that experi-ence to break this cycle and be the driver of change.

In my coaching world, I break feedback into two spe-cific areas. The first is formal feedback, which includes the dreaded annual performance review. The buildup for both parties, the person giving and the person receiving it, can be excruciating. This frustrating experience rarely leads to any substantial improvements. The second type of feedback is on-going, which fuels performance. Continuous feedback is de-livered up, down, and across the organization. And it can be both positive and negative. Do not wait for that once-a-year opportunity if you want to see a fundamental shift in your team's performance.

An example of an ongoing feedback process is known as a "hot debrief." Ask every team member how a client meeting went, and ban the response "Okay." Find out what they heard and where they perceived that the team struggled. In a cul-ture of strong feedback, these debriefs will be well received. If there is a reluctance to participate in hot debriefs, you know you have work to do. Your team won't get better without them. In the military, we had hot debriefs constantly. It was how we strived to pursue excellence at every juncture. It's not used to blame people or point fingers. It's a way of looking at how we do things and making them better the next time.

One of the places I saw this feedback method used most effectively was with pilots. Every time a pilot lands back at base or on the ship, there is a debrief. Undoubtedly, we can all learn things or improve on something all the time—no one is exempt. One of my closest friends, Dan, a former pilot on the Commando helicopter squadron who then went on to fly the Sea Harrier fighter jet, told me how he grew to welcome constant feedback. "I was arrogant when I first started," he said. "I beat thousands of people to start training. I was built up to be super confident."

However, when the flying started, the critique began too. "I realized that if I wanted to make it to the end of the program, I had to accept feedback positively," Dan continued. "Suddenly, I was being told day after day, hour after hour, that I could do things better." He received feedback that he was "scraping his way through" and that there were several areas in which he could improve. This was a shock to Dan at first, as he was so confident in his skill and ability. But he described that sometimes, a one-hour flight resulted in a two-hour debrief, in front of engineers and staff he had never met.

Dan came to realize that the debriefs were not just about peak performance. What he learned could save his life and the lives of countless others. He grew to embrace the courage to admit any time he made a mistake on a flight, no matter how small it seemed. "You hold up your hands and try not to make the same mistake again," he said. "People respect you far more when you accept your mistakes than when you hide from the feedback and never learn."

Poor decisions in finance do not result in life or death. However, inefficiencies that are allowed to fester can result in lost deals, declining profits, regulatory noncompliance, and failing economies. Considering the stakes, isn't a hot debrief worth the small investment of time?

Working together to create efficient operations will also strengthen relationships within a team. As a result, your team will also get noticed. Senior leaders will respect a team that is always looking to do better and achieve more. No one builds anything new by relying solely on past successes.

The point is that to remain competitive in our ever-changing world, we need to question the status quo—which is hard work. In addition to testing things yourself, another way to learn whether you are doing things the best way possible is to ask people you know. Building a solid network will be an asset in your career. Think of each person you meet as connected to a web of other people filled with valuable knowledge and resources. Having a solid network and engaging in thoughtful conversations with as many people as possible will keep a steady stream of ideas and resources flowing your way. If you adhere to the following action steps, I guarantee you will create a culture of continuous feedback, and proactive suggestions will start coming to you.

ACTION STEPS:

✓ Gradually introduce a culture of feedback. Talk to your team about *why* a hot debrief will allow all of you to improve.

✓ Encourage your team to open up by asking questions, maybe about things you noticed during a meeting, and get their opinions on them. Here's an example: "In the client meeting, I thought the CEO tuned out a little when we started talking about overseas opportunities. Did any of you notice it too?"

✓ Pick one of your team members or someone you interact with regularly. Ask them to provide you with two tangible, actionable things you can improve on in the next thirty days.

✓ Be accountable—set about completing the issues they identified.

✓ Make sure you speak to them once you've accomplished the goal, and tell them how the process went and how much you appreciated the input.

R—RESILIENCE

Being challenged in life is inevitable.
Being defeated is optional.

—Roger Crawford (born 1960)
The first person with a severe disability to
play Division I tennis in American history

The ability to keep going and fight through tough times is the very definition of resilience. None of us were spared from adversity as we were locked down during the global pandemic of 2020. Strong mental health and resilience were essential, and we each struggled in our own way. While it was challenging, there were also stories of resilience and redemption all around us. The way we remember this difficult time will shape our future. We can choose to be damaged by it forever, or we can focus on what we learned and how we got through it. We can use these building blocks of wisdom to help us deal with future adversity.

Failures and bumps in the road are part of life's journey. Everyone will face setbacks in their personal and work life as they battle to the top. No one has made it to managing director or any other senior position without challenges along the way. However, how a person chooses to deal with this adversity demonstrates their character and defines their reputation far more than their successes ever will.

There is *always* a solution. Even in the direst of circumstances, with reflection and perseverance, you will fight through. Resilience comes from experience and developing the skills and awareness to make it through difficult times. As you read this chapter, take the time to build your resilience tool kit by being honest about what you find hard or when you feel down. I can guarantee you'll need it at some point in the future.

As I reflect on my journey, I find there have been plenty of roadblocks and disappointments along the way. While I was in the middle of a tough time, it seemed the world as I knew it was ending. As I recall those demanding situations now, I am grateful for every one of them. Each experience taught me something about life, and more importantly, revealed insight into myself. Mastering task after task is somewhat mundane. However, becoming a better, stronger person on the journey is what will make your life matter. The main message I learned from personal hardship is a simple one—*I can get through it.* Regardless of outside circumstances or anyone's opinion, I am confident I will see the other side and things will be okay. It's about realizing and acknowledging when things aren't great, knowing who you are and what makes you tick, and then moving forward through the difficult times.

I attended my first Commando course in the spring of 1999. During one of the early weeks on the course, while on a late-night exercise at the nearby notorious Woodbury Common training area, an elastic bungee cord I used to hold up my shelter suddenly snapped. It whipped around a tree, and the metal hook struck me on the back of my hand. It hurt like hell. My hand began to swell, I started to lose feeling, and I couldn't bend my fingers. I shone my flashlight on the area to look closer and was shocked at what I saw. A three-inch lump had emerged on the back of my hand, and it throbbed with pain. I knew not to argue when I was sent back to camp to seek further medical attention to evaluate the damage.

After a one-night stay in the hospital, I returned to the training area early the next morning with a massive bandage around my hand. I went straight into a four-mile speed march carrying about thirty pounds of equipment. I remember the exercise effortlessly flying by, mainly due to the cocktail of painkillers I was taking. But the injury was severe. I had lost all power in my hand, and I couldn't grip anything. I stuck it out for a couple of days, but the inability to grasp anything was a deal breaker when we were back in camp and on the assault course. I could not continue, and I was heartbroken.

I'd put hundreds of hours into training and securing my place on the course. Now I was heading home due to something as simple and unpredictable as a bungee cord snapping. No amount of training could have prepared me for this freak occurrence.

I had a few miserable days back at my old base. I felt like the world was against me, and I seriously considered not going back. After some soul-searching, I realized I wasn't cursed. I was just unlucky. I had done nothing wrong apart from choosing a crappy bungee cord. These things happen. I decided it was time to knuckle down, deal with the disappointment, and prepare to go again. The doctors told me the injury would take a couple of months to heal fully, but the next course started in six weeks. I had one chance left, and that course was it. When I got back on the course, I was still in pain, and my hand was not fully functional. However, I realized *no one* got through the training without pain, so I committed to go for it.

I can assure you no one has ever put up a shelter using a bungee cord as carefully I did when I returned to Woodbury Common. The others on the course must have thought I was nuts when they saw me carefully extending the bungee and hooking it like the most precious thing on the planet. When I eventually finished the course, I appreciated all I had to go through. Even now, when I recall that time in my life, I remember the hard times far more clearly than the days when things went well. The obstacles were my greatest teachers.

I like to think I've always been resilient; my parents in-stilled it in me. They were good at pushing me to work outside my perceived limits and encouraging me to embrace failure. They guided me to acknowledge what went wrong and think about what I would do differently next time. There wasn't much helicopter parenting in my upbringing. Instead, my parents empowered me to try anything, test it, fail, and get up again. These lessons stand me in good stead today.

But if resilience doesn't come to you naturally or isn't something you've had to think too much about, don't worry—it's a quality that can be learned and developed. We all have challenges and opportunities in our lives; each is a chance to learn and grow, if you embrace it. It is all about educating your future self by evaluating what you have gone through and then avoiding the same mistakes. If the mistakes cannot be entirely circumvented, they can be minimized. The way we choose to perceive any event lies within our control. If you rely too heavily on the opinions of others, you will be at the mercy of their perceptions. So why not allow *your* ideas about what you can or cannot do determine your success?

I have seen people who have handled enormous disap-pointment in their careers bounce back when they calm down and focus on resilience. I have witnessed professionals deal-ing with being fired, missing deals they should have gotten on merit, navigating damaging gossip, working through a crush-ing health diagnosis, and managing home life difficulties. Those who could move forward took the time to objectively dissect each aspect of the situation. No matter how bad a situation is, it's never as bad as we think it is in the moment. Great solutions do not come from a cluttered mind. It's just not possible.

Focus on the situation and start unpacking it. Ask yourself what's true and not true and what's controllable. Avoid ruminating on the worst possible outcome. Doing so isn't helpful. Reveling in negativity does not lead to a pathway out of difficulties. No matter how awful or painful the situation is, choose to look at it differently. Albert Einstein wisely said that problems are not solved with the same thinking that created them. It would have been easy for me to feel sorry for myself as I waited for my hand injury to heal. Instead, after having some time to think it through, I focused on what I could control and continued to move toward my goal. I couldn't do any rope climbing or lift any weights in the gym because of my injury, so I concentrated on other types of training.

Everyone has their way of dealing with tough times or situations. You might speak to that one person who listens and always gives you an objective view. Maybe you go for a walk on your own to clear your mind. When I need to clear my thoughts, I go for a run. I find the act of physical exercise works for me. Find your own way, and when you start to feel the pressure of a situation, remember to use it.

After a difficult situation, start planning some action steps. First, be careful of whom you surround yourself with in challenging times. No one can know precisely what you are going through. Even the most well-meaning people and those who love you can be limited in their thinking. Surround yourself with people who have positive mindsets and can discuss ways to solve problems. These are the times when you will learn what you are made of and who you are.

Second, resilience isn't only something to draw on to help with significant life crises. The qualities of resilience can and should be used in everyday situations: sitting in traffic, experiencing a family challenge, dealing with technical crashes, and—one many of us are familiar with—being trapped at the airport. Use all the tips and tools we discussed in the chapter on EQ. When times are hard, your emotions may go into hyperdrive, but a calm approach will allow you to recover more quickly and even draw strength from the situation.

Most professionals are technically prepared and organized. However, not everyone is mentally prepared to deal with adversity. Let's say you've been working toward meeting with an important client for a month. You and your whole team have worked late nights and collaborated on endless edits of decks. Then, as you arrive at the airport, you feel confident you are on top of your game—only to find your flight has been canceled.

Getting agitated about the situation won't help. Take a step back. Start to define what you can take charge of and be aware of what you cannot. Recognize that your team is watching your behavior. This is a crucial time to demonstrate the qualities of resilience. Many people say they can handle stress, but they blow up when they are challenged or when their buttons are pushed. Will you scream at the airline attendant? Go to the airport bar and start buying rounds of drinks? Bury yourself in your phone? Start complaining and blaming others? Unfortunately, these are all things I've seen happen when leaders are not their best selves.

The action steps you choose to take next are key. One way to handle this unfortunate situation would be to talk to your team and ask them to develop options. Make sure to ask them what they think about the proposed solutions. Be transparent and communicate with the team, your leaders, and the client if necessary. Stay calm and develop a plan. And always make sure to communicate with the client. Some of my clients forget that step, but it's one of the most important. No matter what happens, avoid seeing yourself as the victim. Strive toward being an optimist—a glass-half-full person. It's all in the mind.

MINDSET IS AN IMPORTANT PART OF COMMANDO TRAINING

Four qualities define the British Commando—courage, determination, unselfishness, and cheerfulness in the face of adversity. Those four qualities are plastered on posters and signs all over camp. There is also a particular metal sign hammered into a tree at the end of the endurance course, a brutal test that you must pass to earn your green beret. It says, "500 meters to go, it's only pain," with a cartoon of a fat soldier running along. When I passed the sign during my training, it put a smile on my face, just like it has for the thousands of other Commandos who have plodded past it. It's the perfect message to uplift you during a moment in your life when all you can think of is pain.

Surprisingly, I haven't taken into my civilian life any of the technical skills I learned in my eleven years in the military. But remembering to have courage, be determined, remain unselfish, and maintain cheerfulness in the face of adversity are deeply instilled in me. It seems simple, but being cheerful regardless of the obstacle is incredibly important and a surefire way of showing resilience. Try it.

I remember one dark, cold night right at the end of Commando training. We were on our final exercise and had to march along the unforgiving coast of South Wales. In the distance, we could see some small lights marking the eventual target we would have to attack, but they didn't seem to be getting any closer. We were each carrying about a hundred pounds of equipment. The team was approximately eight miles into the march; we still had a long distance to go, and we were feeling shattered. I remember stopping for a map check when the training team sergeant walked alongside me. "Be a lot easier back in the navy, sir," he said. "You sure you don't want to quit?"

I took a few seconds to think about it. The sergeant was right. I was miserable, my body ached from head to toe, and it *would* be easier if I returned to my old job. But something snapped inside my mind. I didn't work this hard to quit. I knew it would be tough; it was part of the deal. It's why I wanted to be there. Regaining my resolve, I startled the sergeant by breaking into a huge smile and replying, "You're right, Sergeant, it would be a lot easier, but I would miss you too much if I went back." I could see him chuckling to himself as he walked away. At the end of the course, he told me that was the moment he knew I would pass. Mindset is vital in resilience. There *will* be challenges along the way. I promise that facing them with a positive outlook and an occasional smile will help.

This book isn't only about resilience, but it's interesting how it weaves through everything we do. If you explore and apply the knowledge in the previous chapters, you will build your ability to improve your resilience. Here's a reminder of how they can help:

Action—Focus on what you can control, and don't worry too much about what you can't.

Communication—Don't keep things to yourself; make sure to speak to people.

Humility—Ego will destroy far more than it helps. Park your ego and be flexible.

Insight—Build an understanding of how you cope with adversity to keep growing.

Emotional Intelligence—Your triggers will increase under stress. Keep them in check.

Vision—Keep your eye on the target; don't let short-term disruptions get in the way.

Execution—Focus on the task; keep working with your team. They are there to help you.

Resilience—You made it this far, so keep going. Stay flexible, positive, and solution-oriented.

Mindset is the secret ingredient in resilience.

DEMONSTRATING RESILIENCE

A few years back, I worked with a hedge fund manager, Sean, who shared a unique approach he used to select prospective banks. He told me he would put the banks that called on him through the wringer to see how they would respond. In one of the initial meetings, Sean would get angry and call out the bank for wronging him in the past. He would then monitor the bankers' reactions. He wanted to know whether they would crumble under pressure or stay calm and show resilience. Sean shared with me that he knew the relationship would inevitably go wrong at some point. The market would fluctuate, and there was no doubt that misunderstandings would arise in the business relationship.

Every banker *says* they will respond well and calmly under pressure, but Sean wanted to see it from the start. There's nothing like witnessing behavior firsthand. So I share Sean's story with my clients—not so they think every hedge fund manager is putting them on trial when they are angry but to help them understand how sound resilience skills can be a positive thing.

I worked with a talented banker called Alan, who had been passed over for the position of managing director. He was qualified, and the firm liked him, mainly because of the numbers he brought in. But Alan's response to being passed over for the promotion surprised everyone. He had a massive tantrum. He was angry, surly, and challenging to deal with. This went on for months. Alan exhibited passive-aggressive behaviors, including withholding information, showing up late for meetings, and being rude to both juniors on his team and his peers. It got to a point where people didn't want to work with him on deals because of his toxic behavior. The following year, he was passed over for promotion again. This time the reasons were clear. However, now Alan had the additional burden of dealing with the reputation he'd created by his response when things didn't go his way. His situation of being passed over, something that might have been quickly resolved, went from bad to worse.

Shortly after that second missed promotion, I was called in to work with him. Alan's anger was evident when I first met him. He was angry he'd been sent to speak to a coach. He was frustrated with his management; he seemed mad at the whole world. The truth was the company knew he was talented and was willing to invest in him. However, he was in such a state and so convinced that he was right that he couldn't see it. His leaders were doing all they could to redeem him. He was fortunate but couldn't appreciate it, as he was certain he was being mistreated. Alan's talent was unquestionable, but he had no future with the company unless he could pivot.

I started our meeting by letting him vent. I listened to his tales of woe, including how he'd been mistreated. Alan shared that he was more intelligent than the others and was underpaid. He used words like "stupid" and "incompetent" when describing people in other departments he was working with. After listening to twenty minutes of solid complaining, I leaned back in my chair and asked, "So what do you want?"

Alan was perplexed. He turned his rage toward me, shouting, "*You're* supposed to help *me*, not ask stupid questions!" Then he went on to say, "Coaches are worthless. I don't need this, and I need to get back to work!" I broke out into the grin I reserve for such occasions (remember, I said a smile under adversity goes a long way). I don't usually let people throw insults at me, but this was a special occasion. I also like watching people vent their anger; it's always been fascinating to me. "Alan, it's true," I responded. "You are the smartest guy in the room. *But if you're so smart, how did you end up here?*"

This question stopped Alan cold. He wasn't expecting it. Alan was so invested in the idea that he had been robbed that he couldn't see any other options or perspectives. As he was thinking, I leaned forward, looked him in the eye, and said, "We sometimes have no control over what happens to us, in any aspect of life, but we have *full control* over how we respond." I then asked him to describe how he responded to missing that first promotion.

"Not well," he admitted. "I was probably a bit of an asshole. Okay, more than a bit." Then a strange thing happened: he smiled.

Once Alan was willing to listen, we could unpack the "injustices" he'd experienced and build a plan to resolve each issue. I asked him about his goals. He disclosed that he wanted to be a managing director, and he wanted to prove people wrong. Alan wanted to show every naysayer that he *did* have what it took to succeed.

Having a clear vision and a goal for where you want to go are excellent starting points toward building resilience. I worked with Alan to design a direct path to achieving his goals using the ARC (achievable, realistic, and clear) method described in the "V—Vision" chapter.

The first step was to work on his attitude. Alan had to come to terms with the fact that being passed over for a promotion was not the end of the world. Once he accepted that truth, the next step was to address his part in being passed over. On the surface, the easiest thing he could do was change his attitude. We all can choose how we perceive situations.

At first, Alan robotically followed the steps we outlined to get him to his goal of being a managing director. Alan agreed that he would act cheerful even when he wasn't feeling particularly optimistic. He committed to showing empathy to those around him. As he did this, his awareness began to awaken. Alan discovered that not everyone was out to get him.

While Alan felt outraged that his manager required him to see a coach, he agreed to find a way to be cheerful about it and even decided to send her a thank-you note. When he embraced the idea that he could choose to feel optimistic, he realized his manager, Leila, was only trying to help. So with this new mindset, Alan wrote, "Leila, thank you for the investment of working with a leadership coach. I promise I will do all I can to learn how to work in a new, more productive way."

Alan was taken aback by Leila's response. "Alan, I'm pleased all went well. I have every confidence you have what it takes to grow with our company. You have a bright future here." He stared at the computer screen for a few minutes. He wasn't expecting a response like this, so he decided to take action. Alan printed the email out so he could keep it on his desk. He looked at it anytime he needed motivation. It was a reminder that people *did* believe in him.

Most importantly, though, he understood that believing

in himself and his ability to meet his goals would allow him to become an ACHIEVER. He had to own that he could win. Not everyone will be in your corner. When they are not, you need to find the motivation that no one else can touch. Your success is up to you.

Alan was promoted the following year. In one of our final coaching sessions, he shared that it had "not been an easy year." With a big smile, he said, "I'm kind of glad I had this experience. Not getting what I wanted taught me so much about myself." He went on to say, "I didn't learn nearly as much when the path to managing director was clear and all I had to do was follow the steps and do the work." I smiled back; that's how life works.

Charlotte, a director at a mergers-and-acquisitions advisory firm whom I was working with, kept losing deals right at the final stage. Everything appeared to be perfect, but when it came time for the client to decide between the last two firms, her team would lose for one reason or another. Charlotte was spiraling into a dark place, and her pessimistic attitude in those moments of defeat brought her team down with her. The negativity was becoming infectious, and it had started to spread. The firm knew Charlotte was a star who just needed a nudge to get back on track. So she was assigned to work with me to see if I could get her back on a positive trajectory.

At the end of our first meeting, I asked her to write out the situation, detailing what had happened and when. Once complete, I asked her to analyze which parts of the process were within her control. The thought that she could control events created a spark of inspiration in Charlotte. The next time we met, Charlotte had a long list of items highlighting which tactics could be changed or enhanced—and only ones under her control.

I asked her what she did to develop this new awareness. "I stopped worrying," Charlotte shared. "More importantly, I stopped talking about it. Before this exercise, I was focused on all the things that could go wrong." With great enthusiasm, she shared a graph she'd created. "See? I mapped out all that I could influence and control. If it felt out of my reach, I'd start to think about what I *could* do. I created baby steps so it wouldn't seem so overwhelming." I was blown away by Charlotte's strategy and sound processes. I could see why the firm thought she was so talented. All she needed was a little outside perspective, and off she went.

Charlotte involved her team in the review of each lost deal. It could have been a monotonous task, but her natural enthusiasm and drive, coupled with her vision for what it would bring, ensured they all bought in and came with her on the journey. The team identified that their approach was solid, but they did spot opportunities for a few improvements. One example was that they had become a little complacent in describing their firm. The team noted that they'd made the common mistake of "drinking their own Kool-Aid" by assuming what they said made them stand out—but it didn't. The evidence of losing deals in the eleventh hour confirmed their hypothesis.

They agreed that they were smart—but so were all their competitors. The team determined that listing their academic achievements in their bios was boring. Everyone did it. The team decided to customize their bios for each potential client. Everyone agreed on this approach, and now they had the chance to put the idea into action.

The team met next with an athletic clothing company. Rather than listing their MBAs and their prestigious degrees, they listed the sports they enjoyed and added why they liked them so much. These minor tweaks made the difference. No other company had done anything like this. When they met with the prospect, it was as if they were greeting old friends.

The team started positively pushing each other, changing presentations when needed, and testing the messages out on each other. They also committed to having a positive outlook—no matter what. They banned negativity from their meetings. The team started to have fun with it, challenging each other to be positive and come up with solutions. Charlotte's team experienced a complete turnaround—and they started closing new business shortly after. They were much more fun to be around too.

AN ACHIEVER'S MINDSET

How much do you want it? The battle to the top is not easy. If it were, everyone would make it. To develop resilience, you must be determined. Do not allow setbacks and disappointments to define you or your path. As I stated earlier, how you let life's challenges affect you will build your reputation and determine who you are—and ultimately determine your legacy.

Resilience is crucial for you and your team, family, and friends. This is the unselfish component of the Commando qualities. Each time we set our sights on greatness, we demonstrate for others that they, too, can achieve more than they thought possible.

ACTION STEPS:

✓ Expect failure and adversity as a necessary part of life. Commit to dealing with what comes and learning from the experiences.

✓ Check your mindset. Are you open to possibilities? Focus on what you can control.

✓ Compete against yourself. Be better than you were yesterday.

✓ Push the limits of what you perceive is possible. We can consistently achieve more than we think we can.

✓ Remain positive, even when you are not feeling optimistic. Negative words and acting out of frustration will affect those around you. Be a leader for both yourself and others.

EPILOGUE

If you had told me when I first left the military in 2004 that I would end up living in New York and writing a book on coaching and leadership, I wouldn't have believed you. But here I am. Hopefully this is just the beginning of my work on passing down the experiences I have accumulated in my life and career, with plenty more to come.

The eleven years I spent in the Royal Navy taught me a lot about who I am, and I carry those lessons with me through all aspects of my life. I'm often asked whether I would do it again, including the tough times. I always say the same thing: yes, I would—in a heartbeat.

Working as a coach is just as rewarding. It is a privilege to work with all my clients. The people I work with within the financial-services arena are challenging, intelligent, motivated, and fascinating. I learn every day and get as much from them as I hope they get from me.

This book is not meant to be the definitive guide to leadership. Instead, it is a synopsis of my views, compiled from over fifteen years of coaching executives and my time in the military. I hope you can relate to the stories, both from the military and my time coaching.

Change is difficult. After reading through this book, go back and choose one of the chapters to focus on. Try a new one each month. Perhaps you have been told to work on something specific in a review or you consider one of the topics the most important for success this year. Whatever the motivation, concentrate on tackling one competency at a time, and don't get overwhelmed.

I wish you the best on your journey to becoming an ACHIEVER as you win your battle to the top.

ACKNOWLEDGMENTS

This book would never have been written without the help and encouragement of my wife, Heather. She read every draft, pushed me to make each chapter as good as possible, kept me going, and kept me sane in the challenging moments. I can't thank you enough for all your help.

I had the privilege of working with some fantastic people in the military, some of whom have gone on to be my closest friends and brothers. Dan Denham listened and pushed me, in his typical no-nonsense way, to think about things differently, and I appreciate every conversation we had. Rob Segebarth has always been there along the journey to encourage and help. Special thanks to Pete Dawson, Steve Roberts, and Rory Lynch from my old unit, who always kept the faith and had my back.

The book started as an idea in the early days of the COVID-19 pandemic, and I did not realize how much work it would involve. Thanks to everyone who helped me write and publish the book, including Alicia, who helped me put all the words in the right places. And thanks to Reshma and all of the team at Girl Friday Productions, who brought the pages to life and made it look amazing: you've been incredible to work with.

ABOUT THE AUTHOR

Jason Blackwell spent more than a decade serving as an officer in the British Royal Navy. He spent five of those years with the elite 3 Commando Brigade after being awarded the much-coveted green beret. His military career included operational service in Bosnia and the Persian Gulf after 9/11 and culminated in his attachment to US SEAL Team 3 during the 2003 Iraq War, for which he was awarded a Mention in Despatches for combat operations.

In 2005, Blackwell moved to the United States and became an executive coach, later cofounding his own company, Hatwell Group, which specializes in helping business leaders and executives in the financial services industry develop leadership and communication skills.

CPSIA information can be obtained
at www.ICGtesting.com
Printed in the USA
BVHW042308220223
659058BV00002B/20